RETRIEVAL & RENEWAL
Ressourcement
IN CATHOLIC THOUGHT

The middle years of this century marked a particularly intense time of crisis and change in European society. During this period (1930-1950), a broad intellectual and spiritual movement arose within the European Catholic community, largely in response to the secularism that lay at the core of the crisis. The movement drew inspiration from earlier theologians and philosophers such as Möhler, Newman, Gardeil, Rousselot, and Blondel, as well as from men of letters like Charles Péguy and Paul Claudel.

The group of academic theologians included in the movement extended into Belgium and Germany, in the work of men like Emile Mersch, Dom Odo Casel, Romano Guardini, and Karl Adam. But above all the theological activity during this period centered in France. Led principally by the Jesuits at Fourviére and the Dominicans at Le Saulchoir, the French revival included many of the greatest names in twentieth-century Catholic thought: Henri de Lubac, Jean Daniélou, Yves Congar, Marie-Dominique Chenu, Louis Bouyer, and, in association, Hans Urs von Balthasar.

It is not true — as subsequent folklore has it — that those theologians represented any sort of self-conscious "school": indeed, the differences among them, for example, between Fourviére and Saulchoir, were important. At the same time, most of them were united in the double conviction that theology had to speak to the present situation, and that the condition for doing so faithfully lay in a recovery of the Church's past. In other words, they saw clearly that the first step in what later came to be known as *aggiornamento* had to be *ressourcement* — a rediscovery of the riches of the whole of the Church's two-thousand-year tradition. According to de Lubac, for example, all of his own works as well as the entire *Sources chrétiennes* collection are based on the presupposition that "the renewal of Christian vitality is linked at least partially to a renewed exploration of the periods and of the works where the Christian tradition is expressed with particular intensity."

In sum, for the *ressourcement* theologians theology involved a "return to the sources" of Christian faith, for the purpose of drawing out the

D1375615

meaning and significance of these sources for the critical questions of our time. What these theologians sought was a spiritual and intellectual communion with Christianity in its most vital moments as transmitted to us in its classic texts, a communion which would nourish, invigorate, and rejuvenate twentieth-century Catholicism.

The *ressourcement* movement bore great fruit in the documents of the Second Vatican Council and has deeply influenced the work of Pope John Paul II and Cardinal Joseph Ratzinger, Prefect of the Sacred Congregation of the Doctrine of the Faith.

The present series is rooted in this twentieth-century renewal of theology, above all as the renewal is carried in the spirit of de Lubac and von Balthasar. In keeping with that spirit, the series understands *ressourcement* as revitalization: a return to the sources, for the purpose of developing a theology that will truly meet the challenges of our time. Some of the features of the series, then, will be:

- a return to classical (patristic-mediaeval) sources;
- a renewed interpretation of St. Thomas;
- a dialogue with the major movements and thinkers of the twentieth century, with particular attention to problems associated with the Enlightenment, modernity, liberalism.

The series will publish out-of-print or as yet untranslated studies by earlier authors associated with the *ressourcement* movement. The series also plans to publish works by contemporary authors sharing in the aim and spirit of this earlier movement. This will include interpretations of de Lubac and von Balthasar and, more generally, any works in theology, philosophy, history, literature, and the arts which give renewed expression to an authentic Catholic sensibility.

The editor of the Ressourcement series, David L. Schindler, is Gagnon Professor of Fundamental Theology at the John Paul II Institute in Washington, D.C., and editor of the North American edition of *Communio: International Catholic Review,* a federation of journals in thirteen countries founded in Europe in 1972 by Hans Urs von Balthasar, Jean Daniélou, Henri de Lubac, Joseph Ratzinger, and others.

'In the Beginning...'

A Catholic Understanding
of Creation and the Fall

Cardinal Joseph Ratzinger

Translated by
Boniface Ramsey, O.P.

t & t clark

T&T Clark is an imprint of Continuum

The Continuum International Publishing Group Ltd
The Tower Building, 11 York Road, London SE1 7NX

The Continuum International Publishing Group Inc
15 East 26th Street, New York, NY 10010

www.continuumbooks.com

Homilies 1–4 first published 1986 by Erich Wewel Verlag
under the title *In Anfang schuf Gott*
Copyright © 1986 Erich Wewel Verlag
English translation © 1990 by
Our Sunday Visitor, Inc., Huntingdon, Indiana
Appendix first published 1979 by Univ. Verlag A. Pustet
under the title *Konsequenzendes Schopfungsglabens*

This edition, augmented with the Appendix © 1995
by Wm. B. Eerdmans Publishing Co.
255 Jefferson Ave. S. E., Grand Rapids, Michigan 49503
All rights reserved

ISBN 0-86012-406-1

Printed by CPI Bath Press, UK

Gratefully dedicated to
those who heard these homilies
in the Liebfrauenkirche in Munich

Contents

Preface

The human threat to all living things, which is being spoken of everywhere these days, has given a new urgency to the theme of creation.

Paradoxically, however, the creation account is noticeably and nearly completely absent from catechesis, preaching, and even theology. The creation narratives go unmentioned; it is asking too much to expect anyone to speak of them. Against the background posed by this situation I set myself the task, in the early part of 1981, of attempting a creation catechesis for adults in four Lenten homilies in the cathedral of Munich, the Liebfrauenkirche. I was unable then to meet the request of many people to publish the homilies in book form; I had no time to go through the transcripts of them that different persons kindly placed at my disposal. Since then, from the perspective of my new work, the critical state of the creation theme in the present-day kerygma has become so much more evident that I now feel pressed to bring out the old manuscripts again and prepare them for printing. The basic character of the homilies has not been changed, and the limits imposed by the homiletic form have been taken into consideration. I hope that this little book may be the occasion for others to pursue this theme better than I have, and for the message of the God who is Creator to find its appropriate place once more in the contemporary kerygma.

Feast of Saint Augustine　　　　Joseph Cardinal Ratzinger
1985 Rome

Author's Note

For the practical abandonment of the doctrine of creation in influential modern theology I would like to mention here just two significant examples. In J. Feiner and L. Fischer, eds., *Neues Glaubensbuch. Degemeinsame christliche Glaube* (Basil-Zurich, 1973), the theme of creation is hidden away in a chapter devoted to "History and Cosmos," which in turn belongs to the fourth part of the book, entitled "Faith and World." The three previous parts deal with "The Question of God," "God in Jesus Christ," and "The New Human Being." One dare not hope for anything more positive from this arrangement, but the text itself, by A. Dumas and O. H. Pesch, goes beyond one's worst fears. The reader discovers here phrases such as "Concepts like selection and mutation are intellectually much more honest than that of creation" (p. 433); "'Creation' as a cosmic plan is an idea that has seen its day" (ibid.); "The concept of creation is withal an unreal concept" (p. 435); "Creation means a call addressed to the human being. Whatever else may be said about it, even in the Bible, is not the message of creation itself but rather its partly mythological and apocalyptic formulation" (pp. 435-36). Would it be too harsh to say that the continued use of the term "creation" against the background of these presuppositions represents a semantic betrayal?

The same reductionist position, less crassly formulated, appears in *La foi des catholiques. Catéchèse fondamentale* (Paris, 1984). This 736-page work dedicates five full pages to the theme of creation. These are found in the third part, under the heading "Humanity according to the Gospel." (The first two parts are entitled "A Living Faith" and "The Christian Revelation.") Creation is defined as follows: "Thus, in speaking of God as Creator, it is affirmed that the first and final meaning of life is to be found in God himself, most intimately present to our being" (p. 356). Here, too, the term "creation" has completely lost its original meaning. Moreover, in type different from that which appears in the rest of the text and which is otherwise used for lengthy citations or supplementary texts, the "current objections to creation" are presented in four points, to which the average reader (myself included) can find no response in the text. He would then have to reinterpret creation in an existential sense. With such an "existential" reduction of the creation theme, however, there occurs a huge (if not a total) loss of the reality of the faith, whose God no longer has anything to do with matter.

God the Creator

In the beginning God created the heavens and the earth. The earth was without form and void, and darkness was upon the face of the deep; and the Spirit of God was moving over the face of the waters. And God said, "Let there be light"; and there was light. And God saw that the light was good; and God separated the light from the darkness. God called the light Day, and the darkness he called Night. And there was evening and there was morning, one day. And God said, "Let there be a firmament in the midst of the waters, and let it separate the waters from the waters." And God made the firmament and separated the waters which were under the firmament from the waters which were above the firmament. And it was so. And God called the firmament Heaven. And there was evening and there was morning, a second day. And

God said, "Let the waters under the heavens be gathered together into one place, and let the dry land appear." And it was so. God called the dry land Earth, and the waters that were gathered together he called Seas. And God saw that it was good. And God said, "Let the earth put forth vegetation, plants yielding seed, and fruit trees bearing fruit in which is their seed, each according to its kind, upon the earth." And it was so. The earth brought forth vegetation, plants yielding seed according to their own kinds, and trees bearing fruit in which is their seed, each according to its kind. And God saw that it was good. And there was evening and there was morning, a third day. And God said, "Let there be lights in the firmament of the heavens to separate the day from the night; and let them be for signs and for seasons and for days and years, and let them be lights in the firmament of the heavens to give light upon the earth." And it was so. And God made the two great lights, the greater light to rule the day, and the lesser light to rule the night; he made the stars also. And God set them in the firmament of the heavens to give light upon the earth, to rule over the day and over the night, and to separate the light from the darkness. And God saw that it was good. And there was evening and there was morning, a fourth day.   *Genesis 1:1-19*

These words, with which Holy Scripture begins, always have the effect on me of the solemn tolling of a great old bell, which stirs the heart from afar with its beauty and dignity and gives it an inkling of the mystery of eternity. For many of us, moreover, these words recall the memory of our first encounter with God's holy book, the Bible, which was opened for us at this spot. It at once brought us out of our small child's world, captivated us with its poetry, and gave us a feeling for the immeasurability of creation and its Creator.

Yet these words give rise to a certain conflict. They are beautiful and familiar, but are they also true? Everything seems to speak against it, for science has long since disposed of the concepts that we have just now heard — the idea of a world that is completely comprehensible in terms of space and time, and the idea that creation was built up piece by piece over the course of seven days. Instead of this we now face measurements that transcend all comprehension. Today we hear of the Big Bang, which happened billions of years ago and with which the universe began its expansion — an expansion that continues to occur without interruption. And it was not in neat succession that the stars were hung and the green of the fields created; it was rather in complex ways and over vast periods of time that the earth and the universe were constructed as we now know them.

Do these words, then, count for anything? In fact a

theologian said not long ago that creation has now become an unreal concept. If one is to be intellectually honest one ought to speak no longer of creation but rather of mutation and selection. Are these words true? Or have they perhaps, along with the entire Word of God and the whole biblical tradition, come out of the reveries of the infant age of human history, for which we occasionally experience homesickness but to which we can nevertheless not return, inasmuch as we cannot live on nostalgia? Is there an answer to this that we can claim for ourselves in this day and age?

The Difference between Form and Content in the Creation Narrative

One answer was already worked out some time ago, as the scientific view of the world was gradually crystallizing; many of you probably came across it in your religious instruction. It says that the Bible is not a natural science textbook, nor does it intend to be such. It is a religious book, and consequently one cannot obtain information about the natural sciences from it. One cannot get from it a scientific explanation of how the world arose; one can only glean religious experience from it. Anything else is an image and a way of describing things whose aim is to make profound realities graspable to human beings. One must distinguish between the form of portrayal and the content that is portrayed. The form would have been chosen from what was understandable at the time — from the images which surrounded the people who lived then, which they used in speaking and in thinking, and thanks to which they were able to understand the greater realities. And only the reality that shines through these images would be what was intended and what was truly enduring. Thus Scripture would not wish to inform us about how the different species of plant life gradually appeared or how the sun and the moon and the stars were established. Its purpose ultimately would be to say one thing: *God* created the world. The world is not, as people used to think then, a chaos of mutually opposed forces; nor is it the dwelling of demonic powers from which human beings must protect themselves. The sun and the moon are not deities that rule over them, and the sky that stretches over their heads is not full of mysterious and adversary divinities. Rather, all of this comes from one power, from God's eternal Reason, which became — in the Word — the power of creation. All of this comes from the same Word of God that we meet in the act of faith. Thus, insofar as human beings realized that the world came from the Word, they ceased to care about the gods and demons. In addition, the world was freed so that reason might lift itself up to God and so that human beings might approach this God fearlessly. In this

Word they experienced the true enlightenment that does away with the gods and the mysterious powers and that reveals to them that there is only one power everywhere and that we are in his hands. This is the living God, and this same power (which created the earth and the stars and which bears the whole universe) is the very one whom we meet in the Word of Holy Scripture. In this Word we come into contact with the real primordial force of the world and with the power that is above all powers.[1]

I believe that this view is correct, but it is not enough. For when we are told that we have to distinguish between the images themselves and what those images mean, then we can ask in turn: Why wasn't that said earlier? Evidently it must have been taught differently at one time or else Galileo would never have been put on trial. And so the suspicion grows that ultimately perhaps this way of viewing things is only a trick of the church and of theologians who have run out of solutions but do not want to admit it, and now they are looking for something to hide behind. And on the whole the impression is given that the history of Christianity in the last four hundred years has been a constant rearguard action as the assertions of the faith and of theology have been dismantled piece by piece. People have,

1. A good presentation of this exegesis of the Genesis account, along with extensive references, may be found, e.g., in M. Schmaus, *Katholische Dogmatik* 2 (Munich, 1949), 30-39.

it is true, always found tricks as a way of getting out of difficulties. But there is an almost ineluctable fear that we will gradually end up in emptiness and that the time will come when there will be nothing left to defend and hide behind, that the whole landscape of Scripture and of the faith will be overrun by a kind of "reason" that will no longer be able to take any of this seriously.

Along with this there is another disquieting consideration. For one can ask: If theologians or even the church can shift the boundaries here between image and intention, between what lies buried in the past and what is of enduring value, why can they not do so elsewhere — as, for instance, with respect to Jesus' miracles? And if there, why not also with respect to what is absolutely central — the cross and the resurrection of the Lord? This would be an operation whose aim would be, supposedly, to defend the faith, inasmuch as it would say: Behind what is there, which we can no longer defend, there is something more real. Such an operation often ends up by putting the faith itself in doubt, by raising the question of the honesty of those who are interpreting it and of whether anything at all there is enduring. As far as theological views of this sort are concerned, finally, quite a number of people have the abiding impression that the church's faith is like a jellyfish: no one can get a grip on it and it has no firm center. It is on the many halfhearted interpretations of the biblical Word that can be found everywhere that a sickly Christianity takes its stand — a Christianity that is no longer true to itself and that consequently cannot radiate encouragement and enthusiasm. It gives, instead, the impression of being an organization that keeps on talking although it has nothing else to say, because twisted words are not convincing and are only concerned to hide their emptiness.

The Unity of the Bible as a Criterion for Its Interpretation

So now we still have to ask: Is the distinction between the image and what is intended to be expressed only an evasion, because we can no longer rely on the text even though we still want to make something of it, or are there criteria from the Bible itself that attest to this distinction? Does it give us access to indications of this sort, and did the faith of the church know of these indications in the past and acknowledge them?

Let us look at Holy Scripture anew with these questions in mind. There we can determine first of all that the creation account in Genesis 1, which we have just heard, is not, from its very beginning, something that is closed in on itself. Indeed, Holy Scripture in its entirety was not written from beginning to end like a novel or a textbook.

It is, rather, the echo of God's history with his people. It arose out of the struggles and the vagaries of this history, and all through it we can catch a glimpse of the rises and falls, the sufferings and hopes, and the greatness and failures of this history. The Bible is thus the story of God's struggle with human beings to make himself understandable to them over the course of time; but it is also the story of their struggle to seize hold of God over the course of time. Hence the theme of creation is not set down once for all in one place; rather, it accompanies Israel throughout its history, and, indeed, the whole Old Testament is a journeying with the Word of God. Only in the process of this journeying was the Bible's real way of declaring itself formed, step by step. Consequently we ourselves can only discover where this way is leading if we follow it to the end. In this respect — as a way — the Old and New Testaments belong together. For the Christian the Old Testament represents, in its totality, an advance toward Christ; only when it attains to him does its real meaning, which was gradually hinted at, become clear. Thus every individual part derives its meaning from the whole, and the whole derives its meaning from its end — from Christ. Hence we only interpret an individual text theologically correctly (as the fathers of the church recognized and as the faith of the church in every age has recognized) when we see it as a way that is leading us ever forward, when we see in the text where this way is tending and what its inner direction is.[2]

What significance, now, does this insight have for the understanding of the creation account? The first thing to be said is this: Israel always believed in the Creator God, and this faith it shared with all the great civilizations of the ancient world. For, even in the moments when monotheism was eclipsed, all the great civilizations always knew of the Creator of heaven and earth. There is a surprising commonality here even between civilizations that could never have been in touch with one another. In this commonality we can get a good grasp of the profound and never altogether lost contact that human beings had with God's truth. In Israel itself the creation theme went through several different stages. It was never completely absent, but it was not always equally important. There were times when Israel was so preoccupied with the sufferings or the hopes of its own history, so fastened upon the here and now, that there was hardly any use in its looking back at creation; indeed, it hardly could. The moment when creation became a dominant theme occurred during the Babylonian Exile. It was then that the account that we have just heard — based, to

2. Re this and the following, cf. esp. C. Westermann, *Genesis* 1 (Neukirchener Verlag, 1974), 1-103. On reading the Bible from the point of view of the unity of its history, cf. esp. H. Gese, *Zur biblischen Theologie. Alttestamentliche Vorträge* (Munich, 1977), 9-30.

be sure, on very ancient traditions — assumed its present form. Israel had lost its land and its temple. According to the mentality of the time this was something incomprehensible, for it meant that the God of Israel was vanquished — a God whose people, whose land, and whose worshipers could be snatched away from him. A God who could not defend his worshipers and his worship was seen to be, at the time, a weak God. Indeed, he was no God at all; he had abandoned his divinity. And so, being driven out of their own land and being erased from the map was for Israel a terrible trial: Has our God been vanquished, and is our faith void?

At this moment the prophets opened a new page and taught Israel that it was only then that the true face of God appeared and that he was not restricted to that particular piece of land. He had never been: He had promised this piece of land to Abraham before he settled there, and he had been able to bring his people out of Egypt. He could do both things because he was not the God of one place but had power over heaven and earth. Therefore he could drive his faithless people into another land in order to make himself known there. And so it came to be understood that this God of Israel was not a God like the other gods, but that he was the God who held sway over every land and people. He could do this, however, because he himself had created everything in heaven and on earth. It was in exile and in the seeming defeat of Israel that there occurred an opening to the awareness of the God who holds every people and all of history in his hands, who holds everything because he is the creator of everything and the source of all power.

This faith now had to find its own contours, and it had to do so precisely vis-à-vis the seemingly victorious religion of Babylon, which was displayed in splendid liturgies, like that of the New Year, in which the re-creation of the world was celebrated and brought to its fulfillment. It had to find its contours vis-à-vis the great Babylonian creation account of Enuma Elish, which depicted the origin of the world in its own fashion. There it is said that the world was produced out of a struggle between opposing powers and that it assumed its form when Marduk, the god of light, appeared and split in two the body of the primordial dragon. From this sundered body heaven and earth came to be. Thus the firmament and the earth were produced from the sundered body of the dead dragon, but from its blood Marduk fashioned human beings. It is a foreboding picture of the world and of humankind that we encounter here: The world is a dragon's body, and human beings have dragon's blood in them. At the very origin of the world lurks something sinister, and in the deepest part of humankind there lies something rebellious, demonic, and evil. In this view of things only a dictator, the king of

Babylon, who is the representative of Marduk, can repress the demonic and restore the world to order.[3]

Such views were not simply fairy tales. They expressed the discomfiting realities that human beings experienced in the world and among themselves. For often enough it looks as if the world is a dragon's lair and human blood is dragon's blood. But despite all oppressive experiences the scriptural account says that it was not so. The whole tale of these sinister powers melts away in a few words: "The earth was without form and void." Behind these Hebrew words lie the dragon and the demonic powers that are spoken of elsewhere. Now it is the void that alone remains and that stands as the sole power over against God. And in the face of any fear of these demonic forces we are told that God alone, who is the eternal Reason that is eternal love, created the world, and that it rests in his hands. Only with this in mind can we appreciate the dramatic confrontation implicit in this biblical text, in which all these confused myths were rejected and the world was given its origin in God's Reason and in his Word. This could be shown almost word for word in the present text — as, for example, when the sun and the moon are referred to as lamps that God has hung in the sky for the measurement of time. To the people of

3. The text of Enuma Elish is translated by E. A. Speiser in J. B. Pritchard, *Ancient Near Eastern Texts Relating to the Old Testament,* 2nd rev. ed. (Princeton, 1955), 60-72.

that age it must have seemed a terrible sacrilege to designate the great gods sun and moon as lamps for measuring time. Here we see the audacity and the temperateness of the faith that, in confronting the pagan myths, made the light of truth appear by showing that the world was not a demonic contest but that it arose from God's Reason and reposes on God's Word. Hence this creation account may be seen as the decisive "enlightenment" of history and as a break-through out of the fears that had oppressed humankind. It placed the world in the context of reason and recognized the world's reasonableness and freedom. But it may also be seen as the *true* enlightenment from the fact that it put human reason firmly on the primordial basis of God's creat-ing Reason, in order to establish it in truth and in love, without which an "enlightenment" would be exorbitant and ultimately foolish.

To this something further must be added. I just said how, gradually, in confronting its pagan environment and its own heart, the people of Israel experienced what "cre-ation" was. Implicit here is the fact that the classic creation account is not the only creation text of sacred Scripture. Immediately after it there follows another one, composed earlier and containing other imagery. In the Psalms there are still others, and there the movement to clarify the faith concerning creation is carried further: In its confrontation with Hellenistic civilization, Wisdom literature reworks the theme without sticking to the old images such as the seven days. Thus we can see how the Bible itself constantly re-adapts its images to a continually developing way of thinking, how it changes time and again in order to bear witness, time and again, to the *one* thing that has come to it, in truth, from God's Word, which is the message of his creating act. In the Bible itself the images are free and they correct themselves ongoingly. In this way they show, by means of a gradual and interactive process, that they are only images, which reveal something deeper and greater.

Christology as a Criterion

One decisive fact must still be mentioned at this point: The Old Testament is not the end of the road. What is worked out in the so-called Wisdom literature is the final bridge on a long road that leads to the message of Jesus Christ and to the New Testament. Only there do we find the conclusive and normative scriptural creation account, which reads: "In the beginning was the Word, and the Word was with God, and the Word was God. . . . All things were made through him, and without him was not anything made that was made" (John 1:1, 3). John quite consciously took up here once again the first words of the Bible and read the creation account anew, with Christ, in order to tell us definitively what the Word is which appears throughout the Bible and with which God desires to shake our hearts. Thus it becomes clear to us that we Christians do not read the Old Testament for its own sake but always with Christ and through Christ. Consequently the law of Moses, the rituals of purification, the regulations concerning food, and all other such things are not to be carried out by us; otherwise the biblical Word would be senseless and meaningless. We read all of this not as if it were something complete in itself. We read it with him in whom all things have been fulfilled and in whom all of its validity and truth are revealed. Therefore we read the law, like the creation account, with him; and from him (and not from some subsequently discovered trick) we know what God wished over the course of centuries to have gradually penetrate the human heart and soul. Christ frees us from the slavery of the letter, and precisely thus does he give back to us, renewed, the truth of the images.

The ancient church and the church of the Middle Ages also knew this. They knew that the Bible is a whole and that we only understand its truth when we understand it with Christ in mind — with the freedom that he bestowed on us and with the profundity whereby he reveals what is enduring through images. Only at the beginning of the modern era was this dynamic forgotten — this dynamic that is the living unity of Scripture, which we can only understand with Christ in the freedom that he gives us and in the certitude that comes from that freedom. The new historical thinking wanted to read every text in itself, in its bare literalness. Its interest lay only in the exact explanation of particulars, but meanwhile it forgot the Bible as a whole. In a word, it no longer read the texts forward but backward — that is, with a view not to Christ but to the probable origins of those texts. People were no longer concerned with understanding what a text said or what a thing was from the aspect of its fulfillment, but from that of its beginning, its source. As a result of this isolation from the whole and of this literal-mindedness with respect to particulars, which contradicts the entire inner nature of the Bible but which was now considered to be the truly scientific approach, there arose that conflict between the natural sciences and theology which has been, up to our own day, a burden for the faith. This did not have to be the case, because the faith was, from its very beginnings, greater, broader, and deeper. Even today faith in creation is not unreal; even today it is reasonable; even from the perspective of the data of the natural sciences it is the "better hypothesis," offering a fuller and better explanation than any of the other theories. Faith is reasonable. The reasonableness of creation derives from God's Reason, and there is no other really convincing explanation. What the pagan Aristotle said four hundred years before Christ — when he opposed those who asserted that everything has come to exist through chance, even though he said what he did without the knowledge that our faith in creation gives us[4] — is still valid today. The reasonableness of the universe provides us with access to God's Reason, and the Bible is and continues to be the true "enlightenment," which has given the world over to human reason and not to exploitation by human beings, because it opened reason to God's truth and love. Therefore we must not in our own day conceal our faith in creation. We *may* not conceal it, for only if it is true that the universe comes from freedom, love, and reason, and that these are the real underlying powers, can we trust one another, go forward into the future, and live as human beings. God is the Lord of all things because he is their creator, and only therefore can we pray to him. For this means that freedom and love are not ineffectual ideas but rather that they are sustaining forces of reality.

And so we wish to cite today, in thankfulness and joy, the church's creed: "I believe in God, the Father Almighty, Creator of heaven and earth." Amen.

4. Cf. Aristotle, *Metaphysics* Z7.

The Meaning of the Biblical Creation Accounts

And God said, "Let the waters bring forth swarms of living creatures, and let birds fly above the earth across the firmament of the heavens." So God created the great sea monsters and every living creature that moves, with which the waters swarm, according to its kind. And God saw that it was good. And God blessed them, saying, "Be fruitful and multiply and fill the waters in the seas, and let birds multiply on the earth." And there was evening and there was morning, a fifth day. And God said, "Let the earth bring forth living creatures according to their kinds: cattle and creeping things and beasts of the earth according to their kinds." And it was so. And God made the beasts of the earth according to their kinds and the cattle according to their kinds, and everything that creeps upon the ground according to its kind. And God saw that it was good. Then God said, "Let us make man in our image, after our likeness; and let them have dominion over the fish of the sea, and over the birds of the air, and over the cattle, and over all the earth, and over every creeping thing that creeps upon the earth." So God created man in his own image, in the image of God he created him; male and female he created them. And God blessed them, and God said to them, "Be fruitful and multiply, and fill the earth and subdue it; and have dominion over the fish of the sea and over the birds of the air and over every living thing that moves upon the earth." And God said, "Behold, I have given you every plant yielding seed which is upon the face of all the earth, and every tree with seed in its fruit; you shall have them for food. And to every beast of the earth, and to every bird of the air, and to everything that creeps on the earth, everything that has the breath of life, I have given every green plant for food." And it was so. And God saw everything that he had made, and behold, it was very good. And there was evening and there was morning, a sixth day. Thus the heavens and the earth were finished, and all the host of them. And on the seventh day God finished his work which he had done, and he rested on the seventh day from all his work which he had done. So God blessed the seventh day and hallowed it, because on it God rested from all his work which he had done in creation. These are the generations of the heavens and the earth when they were created.

Genesis 1:20-24

In our first encounter with the Bible's and the church's faith in creation, two realizations became particularly clear. We can sum up the first in this way: As Christians we read Holy Scripture with Christ. He is our guide all the way through it. He indicates to us in reliable fashion what an image is and where the real, enduring content of a biblical expression may be found. At the same time he is freedom from a false slavery to literalism and a guarantee of the solid, realistic truth of the Bible, which does not dissipate into a cloud of pious pleasantries but remains the sure ground upon which we can stand. Our second realization was this: Faith in creation is reasonable. Even if reason itself cannot perhaps give an account of it, it searches in faith and finds there the answer that it had been looking for.

The Reasonableness of Faith in Creation

This insight now has to be deepened along two lines. The first thing to be considered is the "that" of creation. This "that" requires a reason; it points to the power that was there at the beginning and that could say: "Let there be. . . ." In the nineteenth century this was viewed otherwise. The natural sciences were profoundly influenced by the two great theories of the conservation of matter and the conservation of energy. As a result, this whole universe appeared to be an ever-existent cosmos, governed by the unchanging laws of nature, depending on itself alone, and needing nothing outside of itself. It was there as a whole, and Laplace was able to say of it: "I no longer need the hypothesis of God." But then new discoveries were made. The theory of entropy was postulated, which says that energy once used up in a particular area can never be restored. But that means that the universe is subject to both becoming and destruction. Temporality is inscribed upon it. After that came the discovery of the convertibility of matter into energy, which substantially altered the two theories of conservation. Then came the theory of relativity, and still other discoveries were made, all of which showed that the universe, so to speak, was marked by temporality — a temporality that speaks to us of a beginning and an end, and of the passage from a beginning to an end. Even if time were virtually immea-

22

surable, there would still be discernible through the obscurity of billions of years, in the awareness of the temporality of being, that moment to which the Bible refers as the beginning — that beginning which points to him who had the power to produce being and to say: "Let there be . . . ," and it was so.

A second consideration goes beyond the pure "that" of being. It touches upon the so-called design of the universe, the model that was used in its construction. Out of that "Let there be" it was not some haphazard stew that was concocted. The more we know of the universe the more profoundly we are struck by a Reason whose ways we can only contemplate with astonishment. In pursuing them we can see anew that creating Intelligence to whom we owe our own reason. Albert Einstein once said that in the laws of nature "there is revealed such a superior Reason that everything significant which has arisen out of human thought and arrangement is, in comparison with it, the merest empty reflection."[1] In what is most vast, in the world of heavenly bodies, we see revealed a powerful Reason that holds the universe together. And we are penetrating ever deeper into what is smallest, into the cell and into the primordial units

1. A. Einstein, *Mein Weltbild*, ed. C. Seelig (Stuttgart-Zurich-Vienna, 1953), 21. Cf. also my *Introduction to Christianity*, trans. J. R. Foster (New York, 1973), 106.

of life; here, too, we discover a Reason that astounds us, such that we must say with Saint Bonaventure: "Whoever does not see here is blind. Whoever does not hear here is deaf. And whoever does not begin to adore here and to praise the creating Intelligence is dumb." Jacques Monod, who rejects as unscientific every kind of faith in God and who thinks that the world originated out of an interplay of chance and necessity, tells in the very work in which he attempts summarily to portray and justify his view of the world that, after attending the lectures which afterward appeared in book form, François Mauriac is supposed to have said: "What this professor wants to inflict on us is far more unbelievable than what we poor Christians were ever expected to believe."[2] Monod does not dispute this. His thesis is that the entire ensemble of nature has arisen out of errors and dissonances. He cannot help but say himself that such a conception is in fact absurd. But, according to him, the scientific method demands that a question not be permitted to which the answer would have to be God. One can only say that a method of this sort is pathetic. God himself shines through the reasonableness of his creation. Physics and biology, and the natural sciences in general, have given us a new and unheard-of creation account with vast

2. J. Monod, *Zufall und Notwendigkeit. Philosophische Fragen der modernen Biologie* (Munich, 1973), 171 and 149.

new images, which let us recognize the face of the Creator and which make us realize once again that at the very beginning and foundation of all being there is a creating Intelligence. The universe is not the product of darkness and unreason. It comes from intelligence, freedom, and from the beauty that is identical with love. Seeing this gives us the courage to keep on living, and it empowers us, comforted thereby, to take upon ourselves the adventure of life.

The Enduring Significance of the Symbolic Elements in the Text

To these two considerations, with which we have deepened our fundamental understanding of our first observation, must now be added a further step. Thus far it has become clear that the biblical creation narratives represent another way of speaking about reality than that with which we are familiar from physics and biology. They do not depict the process of becoming or the mathematical structure of matter; instead, they say in different ways that there is only *one* God and that the universe is not the scene of a struggle among dark forces but rather the creation of his Word. But this does not imply that the individual passages of the Bible sink into meaninglessness and that this bare extract alone has any value. They, too, express the truth — in another way, to be sure, than is the case in physics and biology. They represent truth in the way that symbols do — just as, for example, a Gothic window gives us a deep insight into reality, thanks to the effects of light that it produces and to the figures that it portrays.

I would like to seize upon two elements here. The first is that the biblical creation account is marked by numbers that reproduce not the mathematical structure of the universe but the inner design of its fabric, so to say, or rather the idea according to which it was constructed. There the numbers three, four, seven, and ten dominate. The words "God said" appear ten times in the creation account. In this way the creation narrative anticipates the Ten Commandments. This makes us realize that these Ten Commandments are, as it were, an echo of the creation; they are not arbitrary inventions for the purpose of erecting barriers to human freedom but signs pointing to the spirit, the language, and the meaning of creation; they are a translation of the language of the universe, a translation of God's logic, which constructed the universe. The number that governs the whole is seven; in the scheme of seven days it permeates the whole in a way that cannot be overlooked. This is the number of a phase of the moon, and thus we are told throughout this account that the rhythm of our heavenly neighbor also sounds the rhythm of our human life. It becomes clear that we human beings are not bounded by the limits of our own little "I" but that we are part of the rhythm of the universe, that we too, so to speak, assimilate the heavenly rhythm and movement in our own bodies and thus, thanks to this interlinking, are fitted into the logic of the universe. In the Bible this thought goes still further. It lets us know that the rhythm of the heavenly bodies is, more profoundly, a way of expressing the rhythm of the heart and the rhythm of God's love, which manifests itself there.[3]

Creation and Worship

With this we have arrived at the second symbolic element in the creation account about which I wanted to make some comments. For here we encounter not merely the rhythm of the seven and its cosmic significance. This rhythm is itself at the service of a still deeper meaning: Creation is oriented to the sabbath, which is the sign of the covenant between God and humankind. In a short while we shall have to reflect more closely on this, but for the time being, as a first step, we can draw this conclusion: Creation is designed in such a way that it is oriented to worship. It fulfills its purpose and assumes its significance when it is lived, ever new, with a view to worship.

3. For the exegesis of the Genesis account, in addition to C. Westermann, *Genesis 1* (Neukirchen, 1974), 1-103; cf. esp. G. von Rad, *Genesis: A Commentary*, trans. J. H. Marks, 3rd rev. ed. (Philadelphia, 1972) and also J. Scharbert, *Genesis I-II* (Würzburg, 1983).

Creation exists for the sake of worship. As Saint Benedict said in his Rule: *Operi Dei nihil praeponatur* — "Nothing must be put before the service of God." This is not the expression of an otherworldly piety but a clear and sober translation of the creation account and of the message that it bears for our lives. The true center, the power that moves and shapes from within in the rhythm of the stars and of our lives, is worship. Our life's rhythm moves in proper measure when it is caught up in this.

Ultimately every people has known this. The creation accounts of all civilizations point to the fact that the universe exists for worship and for the glorification of God. This cultural unity with respect to the deepest human questions is something very precious. In my conversations with African and Asian bishops, particularly at episcopal synods, it becomes clear to me time and time again, often in striking ways, how there is in the great traditions of the peoples a oneness on the deepest level with biblical faith. In these traditions there is preserved a primordial human knowledge that is open to Christ. The danger that confronts us today in our technological civilization is that we have cut ourselves off from this primordial knowledge, which serves as a guidepost and which links the great cultures, and that an increasing scientific know-how is preventing us from being aware of the fact of creation.

But in honesty we are obliged to add here that this knowledge is being constantly distorted. The world religions are all aware of the profound idea that the universe exists for the sake of worship, but this idea is frequently misinterpreted to mean that in worship the human being gives something to the gods that they themselves stand in need of. It is thought that the divinity demands this attention on the part of human beings and that this worship has for its purpose the preservation of the world. Here, however, the possibility lies open for manipulation. The human being can now say: The gods need me, and so I can put pressure on them and, if I must, force them. Out of the pure relationship of love, which is what worship is supposed to be, there develops the manipulative attempt to seize control of the world, and thus worship can lead to a debasing of the world and of the human person. The Bible, to be sure, could take up the fundamental notion of the universe as existing for the sake of worship, but at the same time it had to purify it. This idea is to be found there, as has already been said, in the context of the sabbath. The Bible declares that creation has its structure in the sabbath ordinance. But the sabbath is in its turn the summing up of Torah, the law of Israel. This means that worship has a moral aspect to it. God's whole moral order has been taken up into it; only thus is it truly worship. To this must be added the fact that Torah, the law, is an expression of Israel's history with God. It is an expression of the covenant, and the covenant is in turn an expression of God's love, of his "yes" to the human being that he created, so that he could both love and receive love.

Now we can grasp this notion better. We can say that God created the universe in order to enter into a history of love with humankind. He created it so that love could exist. Behind this lie words of Israel that lead directly to the New Testament. In Jewish literature it is said of Torah, which embodies the mystery of the covenant and of the history of God's love for humankind, that it was in the beginning, that it was with God, that by it was made all that was made, and that it was the light and the life of humankind. John only needed to take up these formulas and to apply them to him who is the living Word of God, saying that all things were made through him (cf. John 1:3). And even before him Paul had said: "All things were created through him and for him" (Colossians 1:16; cf. Colossians 1:15-23). God created the universe in order to be able to become a human being and pour out his love upon us and to invite us to love him in return.

The Sabbath Structure of Creation[4]

Now we have to go one step further and see how we can understand this better. In the creation account the sabbath is depicted as the day when the human being, in the freedom

---

4. Important remarks are made on this topic in K.- H. Schwarte, *Die Vorgeschichte der augustinischen Weltalterlehre* (Bonn, 1966), esp. 220-56.

of worship, participates in God's freedom, in God's rest, and thus in God's peace. To celebrate the sabbath means to celebrate the covenant. It means to return to the source and to sweep away all the defilement that our work has brought with it. It also means going forth into a new world in which there will no longer be slaves and masters but only free children of God — into a world in which humans and animals and the earth itself will share together as kin in God's peace and freedom.

It is from this notion that the Mosaic law developed, which has as its foundation the idea that the sabbath brings about universal equality. This is extended beyond the weekly sabbath in such fashion that every seventh year is also a sabbath, during which earth and human beings may rest. Every seventh year times seven there is a great sabbath year, when all debts are remitted and all purchases and sales annulled. The earth is to be received back from the creating hands of God, and everyone is to begin anew. We can perhaps best see the significance of this ordinance (which was in fact never carried out) from a brief observation that is made in the Second Book of Chronicles. Already in the first meditation I mentioned how Israel suffered during the exile inasmuch as God, as it were, denied himself and took away his land, his temple, and his worship. Even after the exile people continued to ask themselves: Why did God do this to us? Why this excessive punishment, which God seems to be punishing himself with? (They could have had no idea at the time of how he would take all punishment on himself on the cross and of how he would let himself be wounded in the course of his love-history with humankind.) How could that be? In the Second Book of Chronicles the answer reads: All the many sins that the prophets inveighed against could not, in the end, be sufficient reason for such inordinate punishment. The reason had to lie somewhere deeper, somewhere closer to the heart of things. The Second Book of Chronicles describes this deepest cause in the following words: "The land enjoyed its sabbaths. All the days that it lay desolate it kept sabbath, to fulfill seventy years" (2 Chronicles 36:21).

What this means is that the people had rejected God's rest, its leisure, its worship, its peace, and its freedom, and so they fell into the slavery of activity. They brought the earth into the slavery of their activity and thereby enslaved themselves. Therefore God had to give them the sabbath that they denied themselves. In their "no" to the God-given rhythm of freedom and leisure they departed from their likeness to God and so did damage to the earth. Therefore they had to be snatched from their obstinate attachment to their own work. God had to begin afresh to make them his very own, and he had to free them from the domination of activity. *Operi Dei nihil praeponatur:* The worship of God, his freedom, and his rest come first. Thus and only thus can the human being truly live.

Exploiting the Earth?

With this we come to a final consideration. One particular word of the creation account requires a special interpretation. I am referring to the famous twenty-eighth verse of the first chapter, when God says to humankind: "Subdue the earth." For some time this phrase has come to be more and more the starting point for attacks against Christianity. Christianity, which is said to bear the guilt for the whole tragedy of our era, contradicts itself through the grace-less consequences of this phrase. The Club of Rome, which with its well-publicized blast about the limits of growth some time ago administered a severe shock to the postwar belief in progress, has since then come to see its critique of civilization (which has been widely accepted) as a critique of Christianity as well. It lies, they say, at the root of this culture of exploitation: The directive given to humankind to subdue the earth has opened the way fatefully to that bitter state of affairs that we now experience. In conjunction with ideas of this sort a Munich author has canonized the expression, enthusiastically taken up since he first used it, "the grace-less consequences of Christianity." What we had previously celebrated — namely, that through faith in creation the world has been demythologized and made reasonable; that sun, moon, and stars are no longer strange and powerful divinities but merely lights; that animals and plants have lost their mystic qualities: all this has become an accusation against Christianity. Christianity is said to have transformed all the powers of the universe, which were once our brothers and sisters, into utilitarian objects for human beings, and in so doing it has led them to misuse plants and animals and in fact all the world's powers for the sake of an ideology of progress that thinks only of itself and cares only for itself.

What can be said in reply to this? The Creator's directive to humankind means that it is supposed to look after the world as God's creation, and to do so in accordance with the rhythm and the logic of creation. The sense of the directive is described in the next chapter of Genesis with the words "to till it and keep it" (Genesis 2:15). An allusion is made here to the terminology of creation itself, and it signifies that the world is to be used for what it is capable of and for what it is called to, but not for what goes against it. Biblical faith implies in the first place that human persons are not closed in upon themselves: they must always be aware that they are situated in the context of the body of history, which will ultimately become the body of Christ. Past, present, and future must encounter and penetrate one another in every human life. Our age is the first to experience that hideous narcissism that cuts itself off from both past and future and that is preoccupied exclusively with its own present.

But now we must certainly ask ourselves: How did the mentality of power and activity, which threatens us all today, ever come to be? One of the first indications of a new way of looking at things appeared about the time of the Renaissance with Galileo, when he said that if nature did not voluntarily answer our questions but hid its secrets from us, then we would submit it to torture and in a wracking inquisition extract the answers from it that it would otherwise not give. The construction of the instruments of the natural sciences was for him as it were a readying of this torture, whereby human persons, despotlike, get the answer that they want to have from the accused. Only later, however, does this new way of looking at things take on a concrete and historically effective aspect, and it does this with Karl Marx. He was the one who said that humankind should no longer inquire into its origins and that to do so would be to act foolishly. Marx's intention here was to move from the question of understanding the "whence" of the universe and its design, which we spoke of at the beginning, since creation in its innermost reasonableness attested most strongly and ineluctably to the Creator, from whom we can never emancipate ourselves. Inasmuch as the question of creation can ultimately not be answered apart from a creating Intelligence, the question is seen as foolish from the very start. Creation is of no consequence; it is humanity that must produce the real creation, and it is that which

will count for something. This is the source of the change
in humanity's fundamental directive vis-à-vis the world; it
was at this point that progress became the real truth and
matter became the material out of which human beings
would create a world that was worth being lived in.[5] Ernst
Bloch intensified this idea and gave it a truly terrifying mien.
He said that truth is now what we take it to be and that
the only truth is change. Truth is, accordingly, whatever
prevails, and as a result reality is "a signal to invade and an
instruction to attack."[6] It takes a "concrete hate-object"[7] to
stimulate us to make changes. For Bloch, consequently, the
beautiful is not the radiance of the truth of things but
rather the anticipated appearance of the future, toward
which we are going and which we ourselves are constructing.
Therefore, in his opinion, the cathedral of the future will
be the laboratory, and the Basilicas of San Marco of the
new age will be electrical plants. Then — so he asserts —

5. In this regard cf. my short study, *Konsequenzen des Schöpfungsglaubens*
(Salzburg, 1980).

6. I take my citations from the illuminating book by F. Hartl, *Der
Begriff des Schöpferischen. Deutungsversuche der Dialektik durch Ernst Bloch und Franz von
Baader* (Frankfurt, 1979), 74-80. Cf. E. Bloch, *Prinzip Hoffnung* (Frankfurt,
1959), 319.

7. *Prinzip Hoffnung*, 318; Hartl, 80: "Without factionalism in love, even
with a concrete hate-object, there is no real love; without factionalism
vis-à-vis the revolutionary class standpoint there is merely idealism going
backwards rather than praxis going forwards."

people will no longer need to distinguish between Sundays and workdays. There will no longer be any need for the sabbath, since human beings are their own creators in every respect. And they will also cease to concern themselves with merely dominating or shaping nature; now they will transform nature itself.[8]

Here we find the very thing that threatens our age formulated with the rarest clarity. Previously human beings could only transform particular things in nature; nature as such was not the object but rather the presupposition of their activity. Now, however, it itself has been delivered over to them *in toto.* Yet as a result they suddenly see themselves imperiled as never before. The reason for this lies in the attitude that views creation only as the product of chance and necessity. Thus it has no law, no direction of its own. The inner rhythm that we infer from the scriptural account — the rhythm of worship, which is the rhythm of the history of God's love for humankind — is stilled. Today we can see without any difficulty the horrible consequences of this attitude. We sense a threat that does not lie in the

---

8. Re Basilicas of San Marco and electrical plants cf. *Prinzip Hoffnung,* 928-29. Re the rejection of Sundays and holidays cf. ibid., 1071-72. In general cf. Hartl, 109-46, esp. 130 and 142. Further pertinent material concerning this question from the domain of Marxist thought is to be found in J. Pieper, *In Tune with the World: A Theory of Festivity,* trans. R. and C. Winston (Chicago, 1973), 55-59.

distant future but that encounters us in the immediate present. The humility of faith has disappeared, shattered on the arrogance of activity. From this there is devised a new and no less ruinous view — an attitude that looks upon the human being as a disturber of the peace, as the one who wrecks everything, as the real parasite and disease of nature. Human beings no longer have any use for themselves; they would prefer to put themselves out of the way so that nature might be well again. But this is not how to bring healing to the world, for we go against the Creator when we no longer want to exist as the human beings that he wanted to exist. It is not thus that we heal nature, but rather thus that we destroy both ourselves and creation by removing from it the hope that lies in it and the greatness to which it is called.

And so the Christian way remains the one that is truly salvific. Part of this way is the conviction that we can be really "creative" only if we are in harmony with the Creator of the universe. We can really serve the earth only if we accept it under the aegis of God's Word. Then, however, we shall be able to further and fulfill both ourselves and the world. *Operi Dei nihil praeponatur:* Nothing ought to be preferred to the work of God, nothing ought to be placed ahead of the service of God. This phrase represents the correct attitude with respect to the preservation of creation as opposed to the false worship of progress, the worship of changes that crush humankind, and the calumny against the human species that destroys the earth and creation and keeps it from its goal. The Creator alone is humanity's true savior, and only if we trust the Creator shall we find ourselves on the way to saving the world of human beings and of things. Amen.

The Creation of the Human Being

These are the generations of the heavens and the earth when they were created. In the day that the Lord God made the earth and the heavens, when no plant of the field was yet in the earth and no herb of the field had yet sprung up — for the Lord God had not caused it to rain upon the earth, and there was no man to till the ground; but a mist went up from the earth and watered the whole face of the ground — then the Lord God formed man of dust from the ground, and breathed into his nostrils the breath of life; and man became a living being. And the Lord God planted a garden in Eden, in the east; and there he put the man whom he had formed. And out of the ground the Lord God made to grow every tree that is pleasant to the sight and good for food, the tree of life also in the midst of the garden, and the tree of the knowledge of good and evil.   *Genesis 2:4-9*

What is the human being? This question is posed to every generation and to each individual human being, for in contrast to the animals our life is not simply laid out for us in advance. What it means for us to be human beings is for each one of us a task and an appeal to our freedom. We must each search into our human-beingness afresh and decide who or what we want to be as humans. In our own lives each one of us must answer, whether he or she wants to or not, the question about being human.

What is the human being? The biblical account of creation means to give some orientation in the mysterious region of human-beingness. It means to help us appreciate the human person as God's project and to help us formulate the new and creative answer that God expects from each one of us.

The Human Being — Taken from the Earth[1]

What does this account say? We are told that God formed the man of dust from the ground. There is here something at once humbling and consoling. Something humbling because we are told: You are not God, you did not make

1. The thoughts that are presented in the following pages have been developed at greater length in my article "Fraternité," in *Dictionnaire de Spiritualité*, 5.1141-1167.

yourself, and you do not rule the universe; you are limited. You are a being destined for death, as are all things living; you are only earth. But something consoling too, because we are also told: The human being is not a demon or an evil spirit, as it might occasionally appear. The human being has not been formed from negative forces, but has been fashioned from God's good earth. Behind this glimmers something deeper yet, for we are told that *all* human beings are earth. Despite every distinction that culture and history have brought about, it is still true that we are, in the last resort, the same. The medieval notion characterized in the dance of death that arose during the horrible experience of the black plague, which threatened everyone at the time, was in fact already expressed in this account: Emperor and beggar, master and slave are all ultimately one and the same person, taken from the same earth and destined to return to the same earth. Throughout all the highs and lows of history the human being stays the same — earth, formed from earth, and destined to return to it.

Thus the unity of the whole human race becomes immediately apparent: We are all from only *one* earth. There are not different kinds of "blood and soil," to use a Nazi slogan. There are not fundamentally different kinds of human beings, as the myths of numerous religions used to say and as some worldviews of our own day also assert. There are not different categories and races in which human beings are valued differently. We are all *one* humanity, formed from God's *one* earth. It is precisely this thought that is at the very heart of the creation account and of the whole Bible. In the face of all human division and human arrogance, whereby one person sets himself or herself over and against another, humanity is declared to be *one* creation of God from his *one* earth. What is said at the beginning is then repeated after the Flood: in the great genealogy of Genesis 10 the same thought reappears — namely, that there is only *one* humanity in the many human beings. The Bible says a decisive "no" to all racism and to every human division.

Image of God

But in order for the human being to exist there must be a second element as well. The basic material is earth; from this the human being comes into existence after God has breathed his breath into the nostrils of the body that was formed from it. The divine reality enters in here. The first creation account, which we considered in our previous meditations, says the same thing by way of another and more deeply reflective image. It says that the human being is created in God's image and likeness (cf. Genesis 1:26-27). In the human being heaven and earth touch one another.

In the human being God enters into his creation; the human being is directly related to God. The human being is called by him. God's words in the Old Testament are valid for every individual human being: "I call you by name and you are mine." Each human being is known by God and loved by him. Each is willed by God, and each is God's image. Precisely in this consists the deeper and greater unity of humankind — that each of us, each individual human being, realizes the *one* project of God and has his or her origin in the same creative idea of God. Hence the Bible says that whoever violates a human being violates God's property (cf. Genesis 9:5). Human life stands under God's special protection, because each human being, however wretched or exalted he or she may be, however sick or suffering, however good-for-nothing or important, whether born or unborn, whether incurably ill or radiant with health — each one bears God's breath in himself or herself, each one is God's image. This is the deepest reason for the inviolability of human dignity, and upon it is founded ultimately every civilization. When the human person is no longer seen as standing under God's protection and bearing God's breath, then the human being begins to be viewed in utilitarian fashion. It is then that the barbarity appears that tramples upon human dignity. And vice versa: When this is seen, then a high degree of spirituality and morality is plainly evident.

45

The fate of all of us depends on whether this moral dignity of the human person can be defended in the world of technology, with all its possibilities. For here a particular temptation exists for our technical scientific age. The technical and scientific attitude has produced a particular kind of certitude — namely, that which can be corroborated by way of experiment and mathematical formula. This has given humankind a certain freedom from anxiety and superstition, a certain power over the world. But now there is a temptation to view as reasonable and therefore as serious only what can be corroborated through experiment and computation. This means that the moral and the holy no longer count for anything. They are considered to belong to the domain of what must be transcended, of the irrational. But whenever the human being does this, whenever we base ethics on physics, we extinguish what is particularly human, and we no longer liberate the human being but crush him or her. We must ourselves recognize what Kant recognized and knew perfectly well — that there are two kinds of reason, as he says: a theoretical and a practical reason. We may call them the physical-natural scientific and the moral-religious reason. It is improper to refer to the moral reason as gross unreason and superstition simply because its contours and the scope of its knowledge are not mathematical. It is in fact the more fundamental of the two reasons, and it alone can preserve the human dimensions of

46

both the natural sciences and technology and also prevent them from destroying humankind. Kant spoke of a preeminence of the practical over the theoretical reason and of the fact that what is more important, more profound, and more determinative is recognized by the moral reason of the human being in his moral freedom. For it is there, we must add, that we image God and there that we are more than "earth."[2]

Let us take this further. The essence of an image consists in the fact that it represents something. When I see it I recognize, for example, the person whom it represents, or the landscape, or whatever. It points to something beyond itself. Thus the property of an image is not to be merely what it itself is — for example, oil, canvas, and frame. Its nature as an image has to do with the fact that it goes beyond itself and that it manifests something that it itself is not. Thus the image of God means, first of all, that human beings cannot be closed in on themselves. Human beings who attempt this betray themselves. To be the image of God implies relationality. It is the dynamic that sets the human being in motion toward the totally Other. Hence it means the capacity for relationship; it is the human capacity for God. Human beings are, as a con-

2. On this cf. M. Kriele, *Befreiung und politische Aufklärung* (Freiburg, 1980), esp. 72-107.

sequence, most profoundly human when they step out of themselves and become capable of addressing God on familiar terms. Indeed, to the question as to what distinguishes the human being from an animal, as to what is specifically different about human beings, the answer has to be that they are the beings that God made capable of thinking and praying. They are most profoundly themselves when they discover their relation to their Creator. Therefore the image of God also means that human persons are beings of word and of love, beings moving toward Another, oriented to giving themselves to the Other and only truly receiving themselves back in real self-giving.

Holy Scripture enables us to go a still further step if we again follow our basic rule — namely, that we must read the Old and New Testaments together and that only in the New is the deepest meaning of the Old to be found. In the New Testament Christ is referred to as the second Adam, as the definitive Adam, and as the image of God (cf., e.g., 1 Corinthians 15:44-48; Colossians 1:15). This means that in him alone appears the complete answer to the question about what the human being is. In him alone appears the deepest meaning of what is for the present a rough draft. He is the definitive human being, and creation is, as it were, a preliminary sketch that points to him. Thus we can say that human persons are the beings who can be Jesus Christ's brothers or sisters. Human beings are the creatures that can be one with Christ and thereby be one with God himself. Hence this relationship of creature to Christ, of the first to the second Adam, signifies that human persons are beings en route, beings characterized by transition. They are not yet themselves; they must ultimately become themselves. Here in the midst of our thoughts on creation there suddenly appears the Easter mystery, the mystery of the grain of wheat that has died. Human beings must die with Christ like a grain of wheat in order truly to rise, to stand erect, to be themselves (cf. John 12:24). Human persons are not to be understood merely from the perspective of their past histories or from that isolated moment that we refer to as the present. They are oriented toward their future, and only it permits who they really are to appear completely (cf. 1 John 3:2). We must always see in other human beings persons with whom we shall one day share God's joy. We must look upon them as persons who are called, together with us, to be members of the Body of Christ, with whom we shall one day sit at table with Abraham, Isaac, and Jacob, and with Christ himself, as their brothers and sisters, as the brothers and sisters of Christ, and as the children of God.

Creation and Evolution

All of this is well and good, one might say, but is it not
ultimately disproved by our scientific knowledge of how the
human being evolved from the animal kingdom? Now, more
reflective spirits have long been aware that there is no either-or
here. We cannot say: creation *or* evolution, inasmuch as these
two things respond to two different realities. The story of the
dust of the earth and the breath of God, which we just heard,
does not in fact explain how human persons come to be but
rather what they are. It explains their inmost origin and casts
light on the project that they are. And, vice versa, the theory of
evolution seeks to understand and describe biological develop-
ments. But in so doing it cannot explain where the "project" of
human persons comes from, nor their inner origin, nor their
particular nature. To that extent we are faced here with two
complementary — rather than mutually exclusive — realities.

But let us look a little closer, because here, too, the
progress of thought in the last two decades helps us to grasp
anew the inner unity of creation and evolution and of faith
and reason. It was a particular characteristic of the nineteenth
century to appreciate the historicity of all things and the fact
that they came into existence. It perceived that things that we
used to consider as unchanging and immutable were the
product of a long process of becoming. This was true not
only in the realm of the human but also in that of nature. It

became evident that the universe was not something like a huge box into which everything was put in a finished state, but that it was comparable instead to a living, growing tree that gradually lifts its branches higher and higher to the sky. This common view was and is frequently interpreted in bizarre fashion, but as research advances it is becoming clearer how it is to be correctly understood.

I would like to say something very briefly here with reference to Jacques Monod, whose testimony should certainly have great value, since he is on the one hand a highly regarded scientist and on the other a determined opponent of faith in creation.[3]

3. I am aware that since the appearance of Monod's book not only has the debate continued but there has taken place an explosion of new publications on this subject, pursuing the most different lines and based on new empirical data, but especially with new theoretical positions. To restrict myself only to German publications, I would mention here M. Eigen and R. Winkler, *Das Spiel* (Munich, 1975); R. Riedl, *Strategie der Genesis* (Munich, 1976); idem, *Biologie der Erkenntnis* (Berlin, 1979); R. Spaemann and R. Löw, *Die Frage Wozu?* (Munich, 1981); R. Spaemann, R. Koslowski, and R. Löw, eds., *Evolutionstheorie und menschliches Selbstverständnis* (*Civitas Resultate*, 6 [1984]). In these homilies there could obviously be no discussion of scientific details but only an exposition of the basic lines of the point at issue and of the limits and relation of the individual methods and of the levels of knowledge corresponding to the different sciences. But in this respect Monod's book still seems to me, by reason of the precision and clarity of its argumentation, to offer the best point of departure. In my opinion, none of the publications that have followed it have approached it in terms of methodological rigor regarding the relationship between the empirical and the philosophical.

Two important and fundamental precisions, which he mentions, seem significant to me to begin with. The first is to the effect that not only what is necessary actually exists. Contrary to the thinking of both Laplace and Hegel, all things in the universe cannot be derived from one another with ineluctable necessity. There is no single all-embracing formula from which everything necessarily derives. According to Monod, there is in the universe not only necessity but also chance. As Christians we would go further and say that there is freedom. In any event, Monod indicates that two realities in particular did not have to exist but could have existed. One of these is life. According to the laws of physics, it could have evolved but did not have to. Indeed, he adds that it was highly unlikely that it would have come about; the mathematical probability was close to zero. Thus one may well assume that this development — the occurrence of life — happened only once, and that this one time was on our earth.[4]

The second thing that could have existed but that did not have to is the human being. This, too, is so unlikely that Monod, as a natural scientist, claims that on the scale of probability there must have been only one possibility for the coming into existence of this being. We are, he says, the result of chance. It is as if we had drawn a lucky number

4. Cf. Monod, 56ff., 178-79.

in the lottery and had suddenly and unexpectedly won a billion dollars.[5] In his atheistic parlance Monod has expressed anew what the faith over the centuries has referred to as the "contingence" of the human person, which, then, from faith became prayer: I did not have to exist but I do exist, and you, O God, wanted me to exist. The difference is that in place of God's will Monod postulates chance — the lottery — as having produced us. If this were so, then it would be very questionable indeed whether one could declare that this was a fortunate outcome. A taxi driver recently remarked to me that young people are saying more and more: "Nobody ever asked me if I wanted to be born." And a teacher mentioned to me that he once tried to make a child more grateful to his parents by telling him: "You owe it to them that you are alive!" But the child replied: "I'm not at all grateful for that." He saw nothing fortunate in being human. And, in fact, if it were merely blind chance that threw us into the ocean of nothingness, then there would be sufficient reason for considering ourselves unfortunate. Only when we know that there is Someone who did

5. Cf. Monod, 179: "Modern science knows of no necessary predetermination. . . . That [i.e., the origin of the human being] is a further unique event, which for that very reason warns us away from any one-sided anthropomorphism. That is precisely because the appearance of life, unusual and unique as it was, was utterly unexpected. The universe did not bear life in itself, and neither did the biosphere bear the human being. Our 'lucky number' was the result of a random play."

not make a blind throw of the dice and that we have not come from chance but from freedom and love can we then, in our unnecessary-ness, be grateful for this freedom and know with gratitude that it is really a gift to be a human being.

Now let us go directly to the question of evolution and its mechanisms. Microbiology and biochemistry have brought revolutionary insights here. They are constantly penetrating deeper into the inmost mysteries of life, attempting to decode its secret language and to understand what life really is. In so doing they have brought us to the awareness that an organism and a machine have many points in common. For both of them realize a project, a thought-out and considered plan, which is itself coherent and logical. Their functioning presupposes a precisely thought-through and therefore reasonable design. But in addition to this commonality there are also differences. A first and somewhat unimportant one may be described as follows: An organism is incomparably smarter and more daring than the most sophisticated machines. They are dully planned and constructed in comparison with an organism. A second difference goes deeper: An organism moves itself from within, unlike a machine, which must be operated by someone from without. And finally there is a third difference: An organism has the power to reproduce itself; it can renew and continue the project that it itself is. In other words, it has the ability to propagate itself and to bring into existence another living and coherent being like itself.[6]

At this point something unexpected and important appears, which Monod calls the platonic side of the world. This means that there is not only becoming, whereby everything is in constant change, but also permanency — the eternal ideas that shine through reality and that are its enduring and formative principles. This permanency is so constituted that every organism reproduces its pattern — the project that it is. Every organism is, as Monod asserts, conservatively designed. In propagating itself it reproduces itself exactly. Accordingly Monod offers this formula: For modern biology evolution is not the specific property of living beings; their specific property is, rather, precisely that they are unchanging: they reproduce themselves; their project endures.[7]

Monod nonetheless finds the possibility for evolution in the fact that in the very propagation of the project there can be mistakes in the act of transmission. Because nature

6. Cf. Monod, 11-31.

7. Cf. Monod, 132: "It fell to the biologists of my generation to lay bare the quasi-identity of the cellular chemistry throughout the biosphere. This was known since 1950, and every new publication reconfirmed it. The hopes of the most convinced 'Platonists' were more than fulfilled." At 139: "The whole system is completely conservative, utterly closed in upon itself and absolutely incapable of learning anything from the outside world. . . . It is at its very foundation Cartesian rather than Hegelian."

is conservative, these mistakes, once having come into existence, are carried on. Such mistakes can add up, and from the adding up of mistakes something new can arise. Now an astonishing conclusion follows: It was in this way that the whole world of living creatures, and human beings themselves, came into existence. We are the product of haphazard mistakes.[8]

What response shall we make to this view? It is the affair of the natural sciences to explain how the tree of life in particular continues to grow and how new branches shoot out from it. This is not a matter for faith. But we must have the audacity to say that the great projects of the living creation are not the products of chance and error. Nor are they the products of a selective process to which divine predicates can be attributed in illogical, unscientific, and even mythic fashion. The great projects of the living creation point to a creating Reason and show us a creating Intelligence, and they do so more luminously and radiantly today than ever before. Thus we can say today with a new certitude and joyousness that the human being is indeed a

---

8. Cf. Monod, 149: "Many exceptional minds seem to this very day to be unable to accept or even simply to grasp that only a selection made from different discordant sounds could have produced the whole concert of living nature." It would be easy to show that Eigen's theories of play, which attempt to discover some logic in chance, actually introduce no new data and to that extent obscure Monod's findings rather than deepen or elaborate them.

divine project, which only the creating Intelligence was strong and great and audacious enough to conceive of. Human beings are not a mistake but something willed; they are the fruit of love. They can disclose in themselves, in the bold project that they are, the language of the creating Intelligence that speaks to them and that moves them to say: Yes, Father, you have willed me.

When the Roman soldiers scourged Jesus, crowned him with thorns, and mockingly clothed him, they led him back to Pilate. This hard-boiled soldier was openly shaken by this broken, beaten man. He placed him before the throng and asked for mercy with the words: *Idou ho anthropos — Ecce homo*, which we usually translate as: "Behold the man!" As Pilate used them, these were the words of a cynic, whose intention was to say: We are proud of the fact that we are human beings, but now, look at him, look at this worm: He is a man! How contemptible, how little he is! But the evangelist John nonetheless recognized in these cynical words something prophetic and passed them on as part of the Christian message. Yes, Pilate is correct when he says: "Behold the man." In him, in Jesus Christ, we can discern what the human being, God's project, is, and thereby also our own status. In the humiliated Jesus we can see how tragic, how little, how abased the human being can be. In him we can discern the whole history of human hate and sin. But in him and in his suffering love for us we can still more clearly discern God's response: Yes, that is the man who is loved by God to the very dust, who is so loved by God that he pursues him to the uttermost toils of death. And even in our own greatest humiliation we are still called by God to be the brothers and sisters of Jesus Christ and so to share in God's eternal love. The question about what the human being is finds its response in the following of Jesus Christ. Following in his steps from day to day in patient love and suffering we can learn with him what it means to be a human being and to become a human being.

Thus during this Lent we desire to look upon him whom Pilate and whom the church itself places before us. *He* is the man. Let us beseech him to teach us what it really means to become and to be a human being. Amen.

Sin and Salvation

Now the serpent was more subtle than any other wild creature that the Lord God had made. He said to the woman, "Did God say, 'You shall not eat of any tree of the garden'?" And the woman said to the serpent, "We may eat of the fruit of the trees of the garden; but God said, 'You shall not eat of the fruit of the tree which is in the midst of the garden, neither shall you touch it, lest you die.'" But the serpent said to the woman, "You will not die. For God knows that when you eat of it your eyes will be opened, and you will be like God, knowing good and evil." So when the woman saw that the tree was good for food, and that it was a delight to the eyes, and that the tree was to be desired to make one wise, she took of its fruit and ate; and she also gave some to her husband, and he ate. Then the eyes of both were opened, and they knew that they were naked; and they sewed fig leaves together and made themselves aprons. And they heard the sound of the Lord God walking in the garden in the cool of the day, and the man and his wife hid themselves from the presence of the Lord God among the trees of the garden. But the Lord God called to the man, and he said to him, "Where are you?" And he said, "I heard the sound of thee in the garden, and I was afraid, because I was naked; and I hid myself." He said, "Who told you that you were naked? Have you eaten of the tree of which I commanded you not to eat?" The man said, "The woman whom thou gavest to be with me, she gave me fruit of the tree, and I ate." . . . And to Adam he said, "Because you have listened to the voice of your wife, and have eaten of the tree of which I commanded you, 'You shall not eat of it,' cursed is the ground because of you; in toil you shall eat of it all the days of your life; thorns and thistles it shall bring forth to you; and you shall eat the plants of the field. In the sweat of your face you shall eat bread till you return to the ground, for out of it you were taken; you are dust, and to dust you shall return." . . . Therefore the Lord God sent him forth from the garden of Eden, to till the ground from which he was taken. He drove out the man; and at the east of the garden of Eden he placed the cherubim, and a flaming sword which turned every way, to guard the way to the tree of life.

Genesis 3:1-12, 17-19, 23-24

On the Subject of Sin[1]

After the end of the bishops' synod that was devoted to the subject of the family, we were discussing in a small group possible themes for the next synod, and Jesus' words at the beginning of Mark's Gospel came to mind. These words summarize Jesus' whole message: "The time is fulfilled, and the kingdom of God is at hand; repent, and believe in the gospel" (Mark 1:15). One of the bishops reflected on these words and said that he had the impression that we had long ago actually halved Jesus' message as it is thus summarized. We speak a great deal — and like to speak — about evangelization and the good news in such a way as to make Christianity attractive to people. But hardly anyone, according to this bishop, dares nowadays to proclaim the prophetic message: Repent! Hardly anyone dares to make to our age this elementary evangelical appeal, with which the Lord wants to induce us to acknowledge our sinfulness, to do penance, and to become other than what we are. Our confrere added that Christian preaching today sounded to him like the recording of a symphony that was missing the initial bars of music, so that the whole symphony was incomplete and its development incomprehen-

1. For stimulating thoughts that contributed to this homily I am grateful to J. Pieper, *Über den Begriff der Sünde* (Munich, 1977).

sible. With this he touched a weak point of our present-day spiritual situation.

Sin has become almost everywhere today one of those subjects that are not spoken about. Religious education of whatever kind does its best to evade it. Theater and films use the word ironically or in order to entertain. Sociology and psychology attempt to unmask it as an illusion or a complex. Even the law is trying to get by more and more without the concept of guilt. It prefers to make use of sociological language, which turns the concept of good and evil into statistics and in its place distinguishes between normative and nonnormative behavior. Implicit here is the possibility that the statistical proportions will themselves change; what is presently nonnormative could one day become the rule; indeed, perhaps one should even strive to make the nonnormative normal. In such an atmosphere of quantification, the whole idea of the moral has accordingly been generally abandoned. This is a logical development if there is no standard for human beings to use as a model — something not discovered by us but coming from the inner goodness of creation.

With this we have arrived at the real heart of the matter. People today know of no standard; to be sure, they do not want to know of any because they see standards as threats to their freedom. Here one is made to think of some words of the French Jew Simone Weil, who said that "we experience good only by doing it. . . . When we do evil we do not know it, because evil flies from the light."[2] People recognize the good only when they themselves do it. They recognize the evil only when they do not do it.

Thus sin has become a suppressed subject, but everywhere we can see that, although it is suppressed, it has nonetheless remained real. What is remarkable to me is the aggressiveness, always on the verge of pouncing, which we experience openly in our society — the lurking readiness to demean the other person, to hold others guilty whenever misfortune occurs to them, to accuse society, and to want to change the world by violence. It seems to me that all of this can be understood only as an expression of the suppressed reality of guilt, which people do not want to admit. But since it is still there, they have to attack it and destroy it. As long as the situation remains thus — that is, as long as people suppress the truth but do not succeed in doing away with it, and as long as they are suffering from this suppressed truth — it will be one of the tasks of the Holy Spirit to "convince the world of sin" (John 16:8). It is not a question here of making people's lives unpleasant and of fettering them with restrictions and negations but

2. *Gravity and Grace*, trans. E. Craufurd (London, 1952), 64; Pieper, *Begriff*, 69. Pieper calls attention to some words of Goethe in *Dichtung und Wahrheit*, 2.8, where he says that we can "not see a mistake until we are free of it."

rather simply of leading them to the truth and thus healing them. Human beings can be healthy only when they are true and when they stop suppressing and destroying the truth. The third chapter of the Book of Genesis, on which this meditation is based, is of a piece with this task of the Holy Spirit, which he pursues throughout history. He convinces the world and us of sin — not to humiliate us but to make us true and healthy, to "save" us.

Limitations and Freedom of the Human Being

This text proclaims its truth, which surpasses our under-standing, by way of two great images in particular — that of the garden, to which the image of the tree belongs, and that of the serpent. The garden is an image of the world, which to humankind is not a wilderness, a danger, or a threat, but a home, which shelters, nourishes, and sustains. It is an expression for a world that bears the imprint of the Spirit, for a world that came into existence in accordance with the will of the Creator. Thus two movements are interacting here. One is that of human beings who do not exploit the world and do not want to detach it from the Creator's governance and make it their own property; rather they recognize it as God's gift and build it up in keeping with what it was created for. Conversely, we see that the world, which was created to be at one with its Lord, is not a threat but a gift and a sign of the saving and unifying goodness of God.

The second movement involves the image of the serpent, which is taken from the Eastern fertility cults. These fertility religions were severe temptations for Israel for centuries, tempting it to abandon the covenant and to enter into the religious milieu of the time. Through the fertility cults the serpent speaks to the human being: Do not cling to this distant God, who has nothing to offer you. Do not cling to this covenant, which is so alien to you and which imposes so many restrictions on you. Plunge into the current of life, into its delirium and its ecstasy, and thus you will be able to partake of the reality of life and of its immortality.[3]

At the moment when the paradise narrative took its final literary form there was a great danger that Israel would succumb to the many seductive elements of these religions

3. On the religious-historical background of the serpent, cf. esp. J. Scharbert, *Genesis I-II* (Würzburg, 1983), 55, and C. Westermann, *Genesis* 1 (Neukirchen, 1974), 323-28 (which is exhaustive if not in every respect convincing). G. Von Rad (*Genesis: A Commentary*, trans. J. H. Marks, 3rd rev. ed. [Philadelphia, 1972]) does not go much further in his interpretation of the meaning of the serpent, but at 89 he observes very well that the kernel of the temptation was "the possibility of an extension of human existence beyond the limits set for it by God at creation."

and that the God of the promise and of creation, who seemed so far off, would disappear and be forgotten. Against its historical background, as we know, for example, from events in the life of the prophet Elijah, we can understand this text much better. "The woman saw that the tree was good for food, and that it was a delight to the eyes, and that the tree was to be desired to make one wise" (Genesis 3:6). In that religious setting the serpent was a symbol of that wisdom which rules the world and of the fertility through which human beings plunge into the divine current of life and for a few moments experience themselves fused with its divine power. Thus the serpent also serves as a symbol of the attraction that these religions exerted over Israel in contrast to the mystery of the God of the covenant.

It is with Israel's temptation in mind that Holy Scripture portrays Adam's temptation and, in general, the nature of temptation and sin in every age. Temptation does not begin with the denial of God and with a fall into outright atheism. The serpent does not deny God; it starts out rather with an apparently completely reasonable request for information, which in reality, however, contains an insinuation that provokes the human being and that lures him or her from trust to mistrust: "Did God say, 'You shall not eat of any tree of the garden'?" (Genesis 3:1). The first thing is not the denial of God but rather doubt about his covenant, about the community of faith, prayer, the commandments

— all of which are the context for living God's covenant. There is indeed a great deal of enlightenment when one doubts the covenant, experiences mistrust, demands freedom, and renounces obedience to the covenant as a straitjacket that prevents one from enjoying the real promises of life. It is so easy to convince people that this covenant is not a gift but rather an expression of envy of humankind and that it is robbing human beings of their freedom and of the most precious things of life. With this doubt people are well on their way to building their own worlds. In other words, it is then that they make the decision not to accept the limitations of their existence; it is then that they decide not to be bound by the limitations imposed by good and evil, or by morality in general, but quite simply to free themselves by ignoring them.[4]

This doubt about the covenant and the accompanying invitation to human beings to free themselves from their limitations has appeared in various forms throughout history and also shapes the present-day scene.[5] I mention here only two variations — the aesthetic and the technical. Let us treat the aesthetic variation first. It begins with the question: What may art do? The answer seems perfectly clear:

4. On this interpretation, cf. esp. von Rad, 87-90. There are related comments in J. Auer, *Die Welt — Gottes Schöpfung* (Regensburg, 1975), 527-28.

5. The following considerations are based on the careful reflections on the concept of sin developed in Pieper, *Begriff*, 27-47.

It may do anything that it "artistically" can. It needs only one rule — itself, artistic ability. And only one error can be made with respect to it — artistic error, artistic incompetence. From this it follows that there are no such things as good and bad art works but only well-written or poorly written books, only well-produced or poorly produced films, and so on. The good and the moral no longer count, it seems, but only what one can do. Art is a matter of competence, so it is said; anything else is a violation. That is enlightening! But it means, if one is to be consistent, that there is an area where human beings can ignore their limitations: when they create art, then they may do what they can do; then they have no limitations. And that means in turn that the measure of human beings is what they can do and not what they are, not what is good or bad. What they can do they may do.

The significance of this is far more evident today with respect to the second variation, the technical. But it is only another version of the same way of thinking and of the same reality, because the Greek word *techne* stands for the English word "art," and the same idea of "being able" is implied here. Hence the same question pertains: What may technology do? For a long time the answer was perfectly clear: It may do what it can do. The only error that it knows is that of incompetence. Robert Oppenheimer relates that, when the atomic bomb became a possibility, nuclear physicists were fascinated by "the technically sweet." The technically possible, the desire to do and the actual doing of what it was possible to do, was like a magnet to which they were involuntarily attracted. Rudolf Höss, the last commandant of Auschwitz, declared in his diary that the concentration camp was a remarkable technical achievement. If one took into account the pertinent transportation schedules, the capacity of the crematories, and their burning power, seeing how all of these worked together so smoothly, this was clearly a fascinating and well-coordinated program, and it justified itself.[6] One could continue at length with similar examples. All the productions of horrible things, whose multiplication we look on nowadays with incomprehension and ultimately with helplessness, have their common basis here. But in the consequences of this principle we should finally recognize today that it is a trick of Satan, who wants to destroy human beings and the world. We should see that human beings can never retreat into the realm of what they are capable of. In everything that they do, they constitute themselves. Therefore they themselves, and creation with its good and evil, are always present as their standard, and when they reject this standard they deceive themselves. They do not free themselves, but place themselves in opposition to the truth. And that means that they are destroying themselves and the world.

6. For both these examples cf. Pieper, *Begriff*, 38, 41.

This, then, is the first and most important thing that appears in the story of Adam, and it has to do with the nature of human guilt and thus with our entire existence. The order of the covenant — the nearness of the God of the covenant, the limitations imposed by good and evil, the inner standard of the human person, creatureliness: all of this is placed in doubt. Here we can at once say that at the very heart of sin lies human beings' denial of their crea- tureliness, inasmuch as they refuse to accept the standard and the limitations that are implicit in it. They do not want to be creatures, do not want to be subject to a standard, do not want to be dependent. They consider their dependence on God's creative love to be an imposition from without. But that is what slavery is and from slavery one must free oneself. Thus human beings themselves want to be God. When they try this, everything is thrown topsy-turvy. The relationship of human beings to themselves is altered, as well as their relationships to others. The other is a hin- drance, a rival, a threat to the person who wants to be God. The relationship with the other becomes one of mutual recrimination and struggle, as is masterfully shown in Gene- sis 3:8-13, which presents God's conversation with Adam and Eve. Finally, the relationship to the world is altered in such a way as to become one of destruction and exploitation. Human beings who consider dependence on the highest love as slavery and who try to deny the truth about themselves, which is their creatureliness, do not free themselves; they destroy truth and love. They do not make themselves gods, which in fact they cannot do, but rather caricatures, pseudo-gods, slaves of their own abilities, which then drag them down.

So it is clear now that sin is, in its essence, a renunciation of the truth. Now we can also understand the mysterious meaning of the words: "When you eat of it [that is, when you deny your limitations, when you deny your finitude], then you will die" (cf. Genesis 3:3). This means that human beings who deny the limitations imposed on them by good and evil, which are the inner standard of creation, deny the truth. They are living in untruth and in unreality. Their lives are mere appearance; they stand under the sway of death. We who are surrounded by a world of untruths, of unlife, know how strong this sway of death is, which even negates life itself and makes it a kind of death.

Original Sin

In the Genesis story that we are considering, still a further characteristic of sin is described. Sin is not spoken of in general as an abstract possibility but as a deed, as the sin of a particular person, Adam, who stands at the origin of humankind and with whom the history of sin begins. The account tells us that sin begets sin, and that therefore all the sins of history are interlinked. Theology refers to this state of affairs by the certainly misleading and imprecise term "original sin." What does this mean? Nothing seems to us today to be stranger or, indeed, more absurd than to insist upon original sin, since, according to our way of thinking, guilt can only be something very personal, and since God does not run a concentration camp, in which one's relatives are imprisoned, because he is a liberating God of love, who calls each one by name. What does original sin mean, then, when we interpret it correctly?

Finding an answer to this requires nothing less than trying to understand the human person better. It must once again be stressed that no human being is closed in upon himself or herself and that no one can live of or for himself or herself alone. We receive our life not only at the moment of birth but every day from without — from others who are not ourselves but who nonetheless somehow pertain to us. Human beings have their selves not only in themselves but also outside of themselves: they live in those whom they love and in those who love them and to whom they are "present." Human beings are relational, and they possess their lives — themselves — only by way of relationship. I alone am not myself, but only in and with you am I myself. To be truly a human being means to be related in love, to be *of* and *for*. But sin means the damaging or the destruction

72

of relationality. Sin is a rejection of relationality because it wants to make the human being a god. Sin is loss of relationship, disturbance of relationship, and therefore it is not restricted to the individual. When I destroy a relationship, then this event — sin — touches the other person involved in the relationship. Consequently sin is always an offense that touches others, that alters the world and damages it. To the extent that this is true, when the network of human relationships is damaged from the very beginning, then every human being enters into a world that is marked by relational damage. At the very moment that a person begins human existence, which is a good, he or she is confronted by a sin-damaged world. Each of us enters into a situation in which relationality has been hurt. Consequently each person is, from the very start, damaged in relationships and does not engage in them as he or she ought. Sin pursues the human being, and he or she capitulates to it.

But from this it is also clear that human beings alone cannot save themselves. Their innate error is precisely that they want to do this by themselves. We can only be saved — that is, be free and true — when we stop wanting to be God and when we renounce the madness of autonomy and self-sufficiency. We can only be saved — that is, become ourselves — when we engage in the proper relationship. But our interpersonal relationships occur in the context of our utter creatureliness, and it is there that the damage lies. Since the relationship with creation has been damaged, only the Creator himself can be our savior. We can be saved only when he from whom we have cut ourselves off takes the initiative with us and stretches out his hand to us. Only being loved is being saved, and only God's love can purify damaged human love and radically reestablish the network of relationships that have suffered from alienation.

The Response of the New Testament

Thus the Old Testament account of the beginnings of humankind points, questioningly and hopefully, beyond itself to the One in whom God endured our refusal to accept our limitations and who entered into those limitations in order to restore us to ourselves. The New Testament response to the account of the Fall is most briefly and most urgently summarized in the pre-Pauline hymn that Paul incorporated into the second chapter of his Letter to the Philippians. The church has therefore correctly placed this text at the very center of the Easter Triduum, the holiest time of the church year. "Have this in mind among yourselves, which was in Christ Jesus, who, though he was in the form of God, did not count equality with God a thing to be grasped, but emptied himself, taking the form of a servant, being born in the likeness of men. And being found in human form he humbled himself and became obedient unto death, even death on a cross. Therefore God has highly exalted him and bestowed on him the name which is above every name, that at the name of Jesus every knee would bow, in heaven and on earth and under the earth, and every tongue confess that Jesus Christ is Lord, to the glory of God the Father" (Philippians 2:5-11; cf. Isaiah 45:23).

We cannot consider this extraordinarily rich and profound text in detail. We want to limit ourselves here to its connection with the story of the Fall, even though it seems to have a somewhat different version in mind than the one that is related in Genesis 3 (cf., e.g., Job 15:7-8).[7] Jesus Christ goes Adam's route, but in reverse. In contrast to Adam he is really "like God." But this being like God, this similarity to God, is being a Son, and hence it is totally relational. "I do nothing on my own authority" (John 8:28). Therefore the One who is truly like God does not hold graspingly to his autonomy, to the limitlessness of his ability and his willing. He does the contrary: he becomes completely dependent, he becomes a slave. Because he does not go the route of power but that of love, he can descend into the

---

7. On the variations of the tradition of the Fall and on their different biblical forms as well as their non-Israelite background there is some information in A. Weiser, *Das Buch Hiob* (Göttingen, 1964), 113-14.

depths of Adam's lie, into the depths of death, and there raise up truth and life.

Thus Christ is the new Adam, with whom humankind begins anew. The Son, who is by nature relationship and relatedness, reestablishes relationships. His arms, spread out on the cross, are an open invitation to relationship, which is continually offered to us. The cross, the place of his obedience, is the true tree of life. Christ is the antitype of the serpent, as is indicated in John 3:14. From this tree there comes not the word of temptation but that of redeeming love, the word of obedience, which an obedient God himself used, thus offering us his obedience as a context for freedom. The cross is the tree of life, now become approachable. By his passion Christ, as it were, removed the fiery sword, passed through the fire, and erected the cross as the true pole of the earth, by which it is itself once more set aright. Therefore the Eucharist, as the presence of the cross, is the abiding tree of life, which is ever in our midst and ever invites us to take the fruit of true life. This means that the Eucharist can never be merely a kind of community builder. To receive it, to eat of the tree of life, thus means to receive the crucified Lord and consequently to accept the parameters of his life, his obedience, his "yes," the standard of our creatureliness. It means to accept the love of God, which is our truth — that dependence on God which is no more an imposition from without than is the Son's sonship. It is precisely this dependence that is freedom, because it is truth and love.

May this Lent help us to free ourselves from our refusals and our doubt concerning God's covenant, from our rejection of our limitations and from the lie of our autonomy. May it direct us to the tree of life, which is our standard and our hope. May we be touched by the words of Jesus in their entirety: "The kingdom of God is at hand; repent, and believe in the gospel" (Mark 1:15).

The Consequences of
Faith in Creation

G. K. Chesterton was often blessed with the gift of a striking turn of phrase. He certainly hit upon a decisive aspect of the work of St. Thomas Aquinas when he observed that, if the great doctor were to be given a name in the style of the Carmelite Order (". . . of the Child Jesus," "of the Mother of God," etc.), he would have to be called *Thomas a Creatore*, "Thomas of the Creator."[1] Creator and creation are the core of his theological thought. It says something for the thesis that it was only with the full

1. Cf. J. Pieper, Introduction to *Thomas von Aquin: Auswahl* (Frankfurt and Hamburg, 1928), 16. For a detailed discussion of the same issue, see M. J. Marmann, *Praeambula ad gratiam: Ideengeschichtliche Untersuchung über die Entstehung des Axioms "Gratia praesupponit naturam"* (unpublished dissertation, Regensburg, 1974), 205ff., 286f.

intellectual penetration of faith in creation that the Christian penetration of the inheritance of antiquity reached its goal. That is why the theme of creation suggests itself for a celebration of St. Thomas. However, just as St. Thomas and his theology have become distant from us, so, until recently, the theme of creation has been far from central to contemporary theological thinking. In fact, the theme of creation has played only a small role in the theological discussion of recent years, indeed decades.[2] It has seemed a question devoid of concrete anthropological importance. At best it has been discussed as a detail of a current issue: the compatibility of creation and evolution, a question which of its very nature is centered on humankind. Is there something proper to human beings that ultimately can be explained only in theological terms? Or, in the cold light of day, must humankind be relegated to the domain of the natural sciences? But even this question remained on the fringe because it did not seem sufficiently "practical." Theology has been seeking its truth more and more "in praxis";

2. Even years ago, several important works emphasized the urgency of the theme of creation: for example, H. Volk, "Kreatürlichkeit," in *MThZ* 2 (1951), 197-210. For further literature, I refer you to H. Reinelt, L. Scheffczyk, and H. Volk, "Schöpfung," in H. Fries, ed., *Handbuch theologisches Grundbegriffe* II (Munich, 1963), 494-517, and to the most recent systematic presentation of the doctrine of creation: J. Auer, *Die Welt—Gottes Schöpfung* (Regensburg, 1975 = J. Auer and J. Ratzinger, *Kleine katholische Dogmatik* III).

not in the apparently unanswerable problem, "What are we?" but in the more pressing, "What can we do?"

Only in recent years has the doctrine of creation begun to have an unprecedented topicality. Human beings' concentration on "doing," on fashioning a new and eventually better world for themselves, has made the resistance to creation stand out with increasing clarity: God's creation and "nature" are having to defend themselves against the limitless pretensions of human beings as creators. Human beings want to understand the discovered world only as material for their own creativity. Suddenly humans' own creations no longer appear simply as a hope, possibly humankind's only one, but rather as a threat: humans are sawing off the branch on which they sit. The real creation seems like a refuge, to which they look back and which they seek anew.

In a radical about-turn, the Christian doctrine of creation is now regarded as the cause of the pillage of the world. Hitherto creation has been a theme for theoretical reasoning, a, so to speak, purely "objective theme"; now it is becoming practical and can no longer be ignored.[3] Redemption cannot happen without or against creation. Indeed, the question arises as to whether perhaps creation

3. Cf. G. Altner et al., *Sind wir noch zu retten? Schöpfungsglaube und Verantwortung für unsere Erde* (Regensburg, 1978). See especially the contributions by K. Lehmann and N. Lohfink.

is the only redemption. It is becoming clearer that we cannot give the right answer to the question about where we should be. "What can we do?" will be false and pernicious while we refrain from asking, "Who are we?" The question of being and the question of our hopes are inseparable.

Thus the awakening and rediscovery of the doctrine of creation opens up a wide field of questions and tasks that can only be touched upon here. I can only try to set before you a few fragments and merely suggest in a sketchy way how they fit together. This Appendix will be concerned more with pointing out a task to be accomplished than with offering solutions or developing a complete synthesis. If we want to reappropriate faith in creation with its basic content and direction, then we must first bring it out of the obscurity that has just been described in the diagnosis of our current theological situation.

The Suppression of Faith in Creation in Modern Thought

The obscuring of faith in creation, which eventually led to its almost complete disappearance, is closely connected with the "spirit of modernity." It is a fundamental part of what constitutes modernity. To go straight to the point: the foundations of modernity are the reason for the disappearance of "creation" from the horizons of historically influential thought. Thus our subject leads us to the very center of the drama of modernity and to the core of the present crisis — the crisis of the modern consciousness.

In the fifteenth and sixteenth centuries, a drastic transition took place from the medieval to a new state of mind. This shows itself in three different ways, each of which is a deviation from faith in creation. First, we must mention the new philosophy of Giordano Bruno. At first sight, it may seem strange to accuse him of suppressing faith in creation, since he was responsible for an emphatic rediscovery of the cosmos in its divinity. But it is precisely this reversion to a *divine* cosmos that brings about the recession of faith in creation. Here "re-naissance" means relinquishing the Christian so that the Greek can be restored in all its pagan purity. Thus the world appears as a divine fullness at peace within itself. Bruno sees that creation, by contrast, signifies the world's *dependence* on something other than itself. The Christian idea of the world's dependence on this something else seems to deprive the world of its power. The world has to be protected against this threat: it is self-grounding; it is itself the divine. The contingency of individual things is indisputable, but the contingency of the world as a whole is not accepted.[4] In the final analysis, this is

4. Cf. R. Buttiglione and A. Scola, "Von Abraham zu Prometheus: Zur Problematik der Schöpfung innerhalb des modernen Denkens," *Internationale katholische Zeitschrift* 5 (1976), 30-41.

just the aesthetic prelude to an increasingly prominent idea in the modern mind: the dependence implied by faith in creation is unacceptable. It is seen as the real barrier to human freedom, the basis of all other restrictions, the first thing needing to be eliminated if humankind is to be effectively liberated.

In Galileo we see the return to Greece, not in its aesthetic and emancipatory form, but in a reversion to the mathematical side of platonic thought. "God does geometry" is the way he expresses his concepts of God and nature as well as his scientific ideal. God wrote the book of nature with mathematic letters. Studying geometry enables us to touch the traces of God. But this means that the knowledge of God is turned into the knowledge of the mathematical structures of nature; the concept of nature, in the sense of the object of science, takes the place of the concept of creation.[5] The whole of knowledge is fitted into the schema of subject and object. What is not objective is subjective. But only the object as defined by *natural science* is really objective, in other words, only the things that can be concretely exhibited and examined. The subjective is everything arbitrary and private, everything outside of science; as arbitrary, it is unworthy of knowledge. "God does geometry." Determined by this axiom, God has to become platonic. He

5. Cf. H. Staudinger and W. Behler, *Chance und Risiko der Gegenwart* (Paderborn, 1976), 56ff.

84

dwindles away to be little more than the formal mathematical structures perceived by science in nature. Of course, for a time, while the method had still not reached its complete form and the extent of knowledge was limited, the idea of creation continued to exist in the form of a postulated first cause. One may be tempted to say that it was the very idea of creation that had the most stable position in the faith in the sense that the postulate of the first cause showed that a concept of God, an idea of God "made rational," was still valid. However, at this point the fundamental interconnectedness of the elements of the Christian faith makes its appearance. A mere "first cause," which is effective only in nature and never reveals itself to humans, which abandons humans — has to abandon them — to a realm completely beyond its own sphere of influence, such a first cause is no longer God but a scientific hypothesis. On the other hand, a God who has nothing to do with the rationality of creation, but is effective only in the inner world of piety, is also no longer God; he becomes devoid of reality and ultimately meaningless. Only when creation and covenant come together can either creation or covenant be realistically discussed — the one presupposes the other. A mere first cause does not express the idea of creation because it thinks of *causa* in terms of the scientific idea of causality. Such a cause is not God, but just a cause — a hypothetically postulated active member of a series of things that can be postulated in science. The idea of creation is on a different level altogether. Reality as a whole is a question pointing beyond itself. If we are to grasp the concept of creation, we must expose the limitations of the subject/object schema, the limitations of "exact" thought, and we must show that only when the *humanum* has been freed of these limitations will the truth about humankind and the real world come into view. And yet we must not try to overstep the limitations by denying God, because that would also be the denial of humankind — with all its grave consequences. In fact, the question at stake here is: "Do human beings really exist?" The fact of human beings is an obstacle and irritation for "science," because they are not something science can exactly "objectify." Ultimately, science does center on humankind — but in order to do so, it has to go further and focus on God.[6]

We encounter a third and entirely different form of deviation from the idea of creation in Martin Luther. Bruno and Galileo represent the passionate return to a pre-Christian, Greek and pagan world. They want to get back, beyond the synthesis of Christianity and ancient Greece, to something purely Greek; in so doing, they lay the foundation of the post-Christian world of reason. For Luther the Greek

6. Cf. A. Görres, *Kennt die Psychologie den Menschen?* (Munich and Zurich, 1978), 17-47.

element symbolizes the alienation of Christianity. He wants to get rid of it; he wants to establish a pure Christianity free from Greek influence.[7] The Greek element that he tries to eliminate from Christianity he finds above all in the concept of the cosmos, in the question of being, and therefore in the area of the doctrine of creation. For Luther, the cosmos, or, more correctly, being as such, is an expression of everything that is proper to human beings, the burden of their past, their shackles and chains, their damnation: Law. Redemption can take place only when humankind is liberated from the chains of the past, from the shackles of being. Redemption sets humans free from the curse of the existing creation, which Luther feels is the characteristic burden of humankind. I should like to support this idea with just one, albeit very typical, text: "Man is man, until he becomes God, who alone is true. By participation in Him he himself also becomes true. This participation occurs when man clings to God in real faith and hope. By coming out of himself in this way, he returns, as man, to nothingness. For where will he arrive, he who hopes in God, if not to his own nothingness? And whither will he depart, he who departs into nothingness, if not to Him whence he comes?

---

7. First and foremost, modernity is based on a re-Hellenization. Its opposite pole — de-Hellenization — has only gradually gained an epochal significance. The failure to see this is the real weakness of L. Dewart's book, *Die Grundlagen des Glauben*, 2 vols. (Einsiedeln, 1971).

Man comes from God and from his own nothingness, which is why he who returns to his own nothingness returns to God."[8] Grace is seen here in radical opposition to creation, which is marked through and through by sin; it implies an attempt to get behind creation.

In the background to all this, we can detect a particular experience of creation — the kind of experience expressed in the Lutheran-influenced prayer book of the Duchess Dorothea of Prussia. It changes the meaning of Psalm 6 in the cry: "I should almost prefer you not to exist than be troubled by you any longer."[9] In the first place, this is completely contrary to the Renaissance experience of the cosmos. But, for the modern age, the dualism becomes typically one between "divine" geometry, on the one hand,

8. WA 5, 167, 40ff. (cited in W. Joest, *Ontologie der Person bei Luther* [Göttingen, 1967], 246): *Homo enim homo est, donec fiat deus, qui solus est verax, cuius participatione et ipse verax efficitur, dum illi vera fide et spe adhaeret, redactus hoc excessu in nihilum. Quo enim perveniat, qui sperat in deum, nisi in sui nihilum? Quo autem abeat, qui abit in nihilum, nisi eo, unde venit? Venit autem ex deo et suo nihilo, quare in deum redit, qui redit in nihilum.* Needless to say, this does not give a complete description of Luther's doctrine of creation, but only a spiritual aspect, which results from the drama of his experience of grace. In point 3 under "The Concept of Creation in Present-Day Thought" in this chapter, I show how something similar takes place in Catholic circles, albeit with different presuppositions and forms of expression.

9. The text can be found in L. Gundermann, *Untersuchungen zur Gebetbüchlein der Herzogin Dorothea von Preussen* (Cologne and Opladen, 1966), table II. Cf. J. Ratzinger, *Der Gott Jesu Christi* (Munich, 1976), 12.

and a world of intrinsic corruption, on the other. Without the mystery of redemptive love, which is also creative love, the world inevitably becomes dualistic: by nature, it is geometry; as history, it is the drama of evil.[10]

It was Hegel who made the systematic attempt to resolve this antinomy and thereby to achieve the supreme philosophy. Hegel's system is ultimately "a gigantic theodicy."[11] God must not be seen as the eternal self-existent Almighty, who stands facing the evil world for which he is responsible. Instead, God exists in the process of reasoning, which can come into being only in the other and in exchange with it. Thus, and only thus, does God come completely to himself. The whole universe, the whole of history, is, then, this process of reason. The individual moments in the process, in themselves meaningless or evil, find their meaning as parts of the whole. The historical Good Friday becomes the expression of the speculative Good Friday, of the necessity of rising up to oneself after the experience of defeat. The problem of theodicy is thus resolved. "Insight" takes the place of the concept of "sin." Evil is necessarily bound up with finitude, and so, from the standpoint of the Infinite, is unreal. Suffering is the pain

10. Cf. R. Buttiglione and A. Scola (see n. 4), 31: "Modern thought faces the same dilemma as classical philosophy: either God is evil or He cannot be blamed for the creation of the world."

11. Buttiglione and Scola.

of limitation, and when it is taken up into the whole, it is abolished.[12]

For Hegel himself, this position remains largely theoretical and therefore "idealistic" (though his philosophy is by no means devoid of political motivation). Only with Marx does it become a call to action. Redemption is now construed strictly as the "praxis" of man, as the denial of creation, indeed as the total antithesis to faith in creation. It is impossible to describe this in detail here. I should like briefly to mention just two of its features.

1. The individual is taken up and abolished in the whole; the individual is robbed of reality, and sin is replaced by "providence." In other words, only the species counts, not the individual. The instrument by which history operates is the party, which is the organized form of class. The following statement of Ernst Bloch's is a typical expression of the idea: the materialist dies, he says, "as if all eternity were his." "This means he had already ceased to regard his 'I' as being of any importance; he had class consciousness."[13] Individual consciousness is taken up into a class consciousness, where individual suffering no longer counts. All that matters is the logic of the system and the future, a future

12. Buttiglione and Scola, 32.

13. E. Bloch, *Das Prinzip Hoffnung* (Frankfurt, 1959), 1378f. Cf. U. Hommes in Hommes and Ratzinger, *Das Heil des Menschen* (Munich, 1975), 29.

in which humans are redeemed by their own creation work.[14]

2. Creation is defined as dependence, origin *ab alio*. Its place is taken by the category of self-creation, which is accomplished through work.[15] Since creation equals dependence, and dependence is the antithesis of freedom, the doctrine of creation is opposed to the fundamental direction of Marxist thought. Marx cannot deny that it is logically difficult to do away with the idea of origin *ab alio*. It can be abolished only indirectly, in the context of the system itself. The fact that humans ask these questions is just a sign of their distorted situation. "Give up your abstraction, and you'll give up your question." "Don't think, don't ask me."[16] It is precisely here that the logic of the Marxist system manifestly breaks down. Creation is the total contradiction of Marxism and the point at which Marxist "redemption" shows itself to be damnation, resistance to the truth. The decisive option underlying all the thought of Karl Marx is ultimately a protest against the dependence that creation signifies: the hatred of life as we encounter it.

14. Cf. F. Hartl, *Der Begriff des Schöpferischen: Deutungsversuche der Dialektik durch E. Bloch und F. von Baader* (Regensburger Studien zur Theologie, Frankfurt, 1979).

15. Buttiglione and Scola, 37.

16. Karl Marx, *Nationalökonomie und Philosophie* in *Frühschriften*, ed. Landshut and Mayer (Leipzig, 1932), 307; cited here in E. Voegelin, *Wissenschaft, Politik und Gnosis* (Munich, 1959), 36.

And it is this fundamental attitude that, at all times, is the strongest fuel of Marxist thought and Marxist praxis.

The Concept of Creation in Present-Day Thought: Three Forms of Concealment

In the light of all that we have said, the concept of creation can be seen as a crossroads in the course of intellectual history. However, anyone trying to draw attention to it today must first appreciate that, in several very different ways, it is concealed and can only make its impact when the place of concealment has been discovered.

1. The concept is concealed first of all by the scientific concept of nature. "Nature" is understood exclusively in the sense of the object of science; any other definition of the word is dismissed as meaningless. Theological arguments about the "nature of humans" or "natural rights," resting as they do on the concept of creation, meet a look of blank incomprehension; in fact, they seem nonsensical, the relic of an archaic "natural philosophy." The physico-chemical structure of human beings provides no foundation for the propositions of traditional moral theology, nor indeed for any ethical propositions; at most, it allows us to make statements about the limits of what is feasible. Henceforth the moral and the feasible are identical. As a makeshift,

the concept of nature then offers its services to behavioral research. The trouble is, though, as A. Portmann has rightly objected, that this kind of naturalness just does not exist in human beings. He speaks of the "natural artificiality" of the various forms of human society and culture. Whatever aspect of human social life we consider, "from language to the formation of the state, from the order of sexual relationship to the rearing of children, . . . everything is tied up with decision-making."[17] Of course, if the alternative to naturalness as defined by behavioral research is artificiality, and if decision making is the crucial issue, then again the question arises: Where is decision making going to find its criteria? Or are humans "condemned," as Sartre thought, to finding themselves in a formless freedom? If creation cannot be recognized as the metaphysical middle term between nature and artificiality, then the plunge into nothingness is unavoidable.

2. Reaction and resentment against technology, which is already noticeable in Rousseau, has long since become a resentment against humans, who are seen as the disease of nature. This being that emerges out of nature's exact objectivity and straightforwardness is responsible for disturbing the beautiful balance of nature. Humans are diseased by their mind and its consequence, freedom. Mind and freedom

17. A. Portmann, *Biologie und Geist* (Herder, 1963), 266-71.

are the sickness of nature. Human beings, the world, should be delivered from them if there is to be redemption. To restore the balance, humans must be healed of being human. In ethnology, this is the thrust of Levi-Strauss's thinking; in psychology, of Skinner's.[18] At the scientific level, both men express a mood that is more and more widespread, and that, in various forms of nihilism, is becoming an ever greater temptation for the youth of the West.

3. There is also, however, a theological concealment of the concept of creation, which, causally, is probably connected with the two previous concealments. Here nature is undermined for the sake of grace; it is robbed of its belongings and gives way, so to speak, before grace. Here we should recall the crucial text of 1 Corinthians 15:46: "It is not the spiritual which is first but the physical, and *then* the spiritual" (RSV). There is a series of stages that must not be absorbed into a monism of grace. I believe that we must develop a Christian pedagogy that accepts creation and gives concrete expression to these two poles of the one faith. We must never try to take the second step before the first: first the physical, then the spiritual. If we skip this sequence, creation is denied, and grace is deprived of its foundation.[19] A

18. Cf. Gorres (n. 6), 20ff. On Levi-Strauss, see B. Adoukonou, *Jalons pour une théologie africaine* (Forthcoming from Fayard, Paris).

19. Important insights on this subject can be found in M. J. Marmann's work (n. 1). In connection with this problem, he makes great importance as

selflessness that tries to abolish one's own "I" degenerates into "I-lessness," and then "Thou-lessness" follows directly. This undermining of creation can never become a vehicle of grace, but only of an *odium generis humani*, a Gnostic disenchantment with creation, which ultimately does not and cannot desire grace any longer.[20] The Christian concept of love is the very heart of Christianity and the total antithesis of Gnosticism. However, in Christian religious education and in exaggerated theories of what is distinctively Christian, it has repeatedly been made the point at which creation is negated, and so has been turned into its exact opposite. No, Christian love presupposes faith in the Creator. It must include acceptance of myself as his creature and love of the Creator's creation in me; it must lead to the freedom to accept myself as well as any other member of the Body of Christ. . . . The same is true of repentance. It is a way of saying Yes and is distorted into its opposite when it becomes hatred of self.

---

well as real significance of the distinction between natural and supernatural. In so doing, he shows the irrevocable contribution of St. Thomas to theology.

20. I have gone into more detail on this point in my essay "Ist der Glaube wirklich 'Frohe Botschaft'?" in H. Boclaars and R. Tremblay, *In libertatem vocati estis: Miscellanea B. Haring* (Rome, 1977), 523-33. In this context, one must also reject the opposition set up by A. Nygren between Eros and Agape. See J. Piper, *Über die Liebe* (Munich, 1972).

Faith in Creation as a Basic Decision about Human Beings

After all that has been said, we should now be able to define the decisive and distinctive features of the two fundamental options that, albeit with many variations, line up against each other. As I survey all the perplexing shifts in the spiritual landscape of today, only these two basic models seem to me to be up for discussion. The first I should like to call the Gnostic model, the other the Christian model.

I see the common core of Gnosticism, in all its different forms and versions, as the repudiation of creation. This common core has a common effect on the doctrine of humankind to be found in the various models of Gnosticism: the mystery of suffering, of love, of substitutionary redemption, is rejected in favor of a control of the world and of life through knowledge. Love appears too insecure a foundation for life and world. It means one has to depend on something unpredictable and unenforceable, something we cannot certainly make for ourselves, but can only await and receive. What is awaited may fail to appear. It makes me permanently dependent. It seems like a permanent risk factor, a source of insecurity over which I have no control. I can be cheated, and I am completely powerless to prevent it. Thus, instead of being a beautiful promise, love becomes an unbearable feeling of dependence, of subjection. This risk factor must be eliminated. We cannot stake everything on it in advance. All we can rely on is what we can control, knowledge, which gives us power over the world and, as an all-inclusive system, is free from unpredictability. In the Gnostic view of the world, whether ancient or modern, creation appears as dependence, and God as the reason for dependence. This is the very essence of God, his definition, and the reason why Gnosticism can never be neutral in matters concerning God, but rather aggressively antitheistic. The Gnostic option aims at knowledge and at power through knowledge, the only reliable redemption of humankind. Gnosticism will not entrust itself to a world already created, but only to a world still to be created. There is no need for trust, only skill.

The Christian option is the exact opposite. Human beings *are* dependent, and only by denying their very being can they dispute the fact. This is the point at which we must stress the arational, indeed antirational, character of Marxist rationalism. Marx thinks that the question of origin has "become practically impossible" for Socialist people. For Marx, it sinks to the level of mere curiosity. Humans do not need to know their origin in order to exist in their own right. Whether the world was created by God or came into being by chance "is of no importance and has no kind of influence on the course of our life."[21] To this we must

21. Cf. Buttiglione and Scola, 39; Voegelin.

reply: No, the question *does* have influence, and Marx would not take so much trouble to eliminate it if it were otherwise. We must emphasize that here the Marxist system leads to a ban on questioning. It rules out the old basic questions by referring to their alleged sociological conditioning. Here lies the methodical inflexibility of this whole way of thinking, which imposes quite definite limits on rationality itself. Within its self-generated structure, the Marxist system draws a line between allowed and disallowed questions. Human thinking gets dogmatic spoon feeding from the system, but then that is exactly in line with the general demands that the system (the Party) makes on humans.

Let us return to the point of our question. Humans *are* dependent. They cannot live except from others and by trust. But there is nothing degrading about dependence when it takes the form of love, for then it is no longer dependence, the diminishing of self through competition with others. Dependence in the form of love precisely constitutes the self as self and sets it free, because love essentially takes the form of saying, "I want you to be." It is creativity, the only creative power, which can bring forth the other as other without envy or loss of self.[22] Humans are dependent — that is the primary truth about them. And because it is, only love can redeem them, for only love

22. Cf. J. Pieper, *Liebe,* esp. 38ff.

transforms dependence into freedom. Thus human beings will only succeed in destroying their own redemption, destroying themselves, if they eliminate love "to be on the safe side." For humans, the crucified God is the visible certainty that creation is already an expression of love: we exist on the foundation of love.[23] It is therefore a constitutive part of Christian faith to accept mystery as the center of reality, that is to say, to accept love, creation as love, and to make that love the foundation of one's life.

For each of the two alternatives of thought that we have described there is an alternative way of living. The fundamental Christian attitude is one of humility, a humility of being, not a merely moralistic one: being as receiving, accepting oneself as created and dependent on "love." In contrast to this Christian humility, which acknowledges existence, is a strangely different kind, a humility that despises existence: in themselves humans are nothing, naked apes, particularly aggressive rats, though perhaps we can still make something of them. . . . The doctrine of creation is, therefore, inseparably included within the doctrine of redemption. The doctrine of redemption is based on the doctrine of creation, on an irrevocable Yes to creation. The

23. Cf. J. Schmidt, "Ich glaube an Gott, den Schöpfer des Himmels und der Erde," 1-14, and G. Martelet, "Der Erstgeborene der Schöpfung. Fur eine christologische Schau der Schöpfung," 15-29, both in *Internationale katholische Zeitschrift* 5 (1976).

fundamental opposition set up by modernity between loving and making turns out to be identical with the opposition between trusting being and doubting being (the forgetting of being, the refusal of being). The latter manifests itself as the belief in progress, the principle of hope, the principle of class struggle, in other words, creativity as opposed to creation, the production of the world as opposed to the existence of creation.

As soon as we realize what this opposition involves, we see the hopelessness of taking a stand against creation. Even "creativity" can only work with the *creatum* of the given creation. Only if the being of creation is good, only if trust in being is fundamentally justified, are humans at all redeemable. Only if the Redeemer is also Creator can he really be Redeemer. That is why the question of what we do is decided by the ground of what we are. We can win the future only if we do not lose creation.

(Translated by Helen A. Saward)